MUSEUM MASTERPIECES IN NEEDLEPOINT

Books by Brande Ormond

Needlepoints to Go: Small Projects for Spare Moments

American Primitives in Needlepoint

Museum Masterpieces in Needlepoint
  (Text by Marion Muller)

MUSEUM MASTERPIECES IN NEEDLEPOINT

by Brande Ormond

Text by Marion Muller

HOUGHTON MIFFLIN COMPANY BOSTON 1978

FOR GRANDMOTHER LAURITZEN

FOR LARRY
. . . *humanist, philanthropist, supporter of the arts*

Library of Congress Cataloging in Publication Data
Ormond, Brande.
    Museum masterpieces in needlepoint.
    1. Canvas embroidery — Patterns.   I. Muller, Marion.
II. Title.
TT778.C30745   746.4'4   78-18272
ISBN 0-395-27093-6

Printed in the United States of America

M 10 9 8 7 6 5 4 3 2 1

Acknowledgments

I wish to thank my hardworking family and friends for their help in making the original needlepoint pieces to photograph: Marge Gross, Jan Lauritzen, Beka Martin, Betty McDonnell, Marion Muller, Elaine Ormond, Alberta Saletan, Flavia Stutz, Frances Tenenbaum, and Ina Zoob.

Billie Conkling provided canvas and wool for the samples from her needlework shop in Ruxton, Maryland, and I thank her.

Special thanks to Fran Tenenbaum, our editor, and Marion, my co-author.

BRANDE ORMOND

Contents

Introduction

When I was first approached about writing the text for this book, I was somewhat reticent. I knew my reservations grew out of a deep-seated puritanical attitude toward art. I was reared in a school of thinking that carefully distinguished fine art from commercial, expressive from decorative, and most emphatically, *art* from *craft*! Here was the crux of the problem: the combination of painting — a fine art — with needlepoint — a craft.

But because I am a needlepoint addict, and because I am involved with painting in a more-than-casual affair, and because I have enormous respect for the intelligence and esthetic sensibility of Frances Tenenbaum, our editor, I let her enthusiasm sway me. I decided to keep my peace and examine my prejudices privately.

In a very short time — after the first of innumerable hours in museums, libraries and bookshops — I was ready to renounce my cultural snobbism. I want to recant publicly, because I know there are many esthetically sophisticated people who share the prejudices of my misguided past. For their sakes and mine, I would like to clear the air and explain my complete change of heart with regard to the combination of fine art and needlepoint.

My outlook changed when I opened my mind to the simple fact that needlepoint is a textile. In readings that took me back to the beginnings of civilization, I was reminded that the designing and weaving of textiles is an ancient and venerable art. The Egyptians were at it 2000 years before the beginning of our calendar. The Indians of Peru were master weavers even before them. In the Byzantine world, textiles were such a high art form — so rich in design, and executed with such consummate artistry — that crusaders returning to Europe carried them back as fitting gifts for their monarchs. Those textiles were valued as highly as gold or precious gems. In the Western world, the fabulous tapestries woven for medieval courts and cathedrals are among the rarest treasures in our museums today.

I considered the story of the Bayeux tapestry and was forced to ask myself: Would this 231-foot picture-legend of the Norman Conquest of England be a worthier work of art if it had been painted on canvas rather than embroidered on linen?

Would the fabulous Unicorn tapestries be greater treasures if left in cartoon form? (The cartoon is the drawn and painted picture from which weavers work.) The fact is that old masters like Rubens and Goya, and modern masters like Picasso and Braque, all engaged in making cartoons for tapestry design in the course of their careers.

As I reviewed the history of art, I answered my own doubts. In the realm of art, there can be no limitations on man's areas of expression. From the beginning of time, he has recorded his lifestyle, his wishes, his hopes, his fears, his myths and fantasies. They have appeared on the walls of caves, on vases, on the ceilings of churches, on textiles, in manuscripts, and only recently, considering the total span of history, in framed pictures over the couches of the world. A needlepoint is as fitting a surface for a work of art as any man has devised. The artistry of a needlepoint depends on the very same qualities we look for in all other works of art: it should be unique in its concept and excellent in its execution.

With a clear mind and enthusiastic spirit, I happily joined Brande Ormond, the artist and needlepoint expert, in this cooperative venture. We decided at the start that we would include only works of unquestionable artistic merit. There would be nothing insipid or pandering in our collection. And — extremely important — the works would translate into needlepoint without compromising the character of the original.

Even with our high-minded goals, it seemed at first that our sources were limitless. But sometimes our enthusiasm gave way to frustration. We agonized a good deal over a number of stunning works that simply could not be graphed without Brande losing her mind, or you giving up in despair at the execution of such a needlepoint. We had to rule out the magnificent paintings of the Renaissance. Their illusory effects and transparent glazes would be lost in needlepoint. We had to forgo everybody's favorite Impressionist paintings. The myriad dots and brush strokes of color that are typical of those paintings could not be accurately diagrammed. And so it went.

But rather than dwell on the omissions, we know you'll find pleasure in the twelve works we have included. You'll notice that we've chosen works of art that are representative of major colorful periods in history.

From antiquity, there are two designs: a Greek vase painting and a wall decoration from an Egyptian tomb. From Medieval France, we have a page out of an illuminated manuscript. There is an Indian miniature painting from the Islamic world, and a Japanese screen painting from the Orient. From the mid-nineteenth century, we chose an American work by an anonymous painter and, from the same period, paintings by the most famous names in modern European art. We stopped short of using contemporary works of art for two reasons: we did not wish to tangle with reproduction rights of works by living artists, and second, it is too early to tell which of the contemporary works in museums today can rightfully be called masterpieces. So we abided by our original purpose, which was to provide you with the means to reproduce museum masterpieces in needlepoint.

We have learned a good deal in putting this book together. There was much footwork, eyestrain and nail-biting for us. For you, we hope it will be pure pleasure.

MARION MULLER

MUSEUM
MASTERPIECES
IN
NEEDLEPOINT

Instructions

. . . and a few encouraging remarks

At first glance, some of the projects in this book may seem ambitious, and you might think they are geared to highly experienced needlepointers only. Not so. If you can count to ten, you should have no difficulty working from the graphs. The instructions are explicit and easy to follow. Of course, if you've never worked from a graph before, it makes sense to proceed from one of the simpler designs to the more complex.

We would also like to encourage you not to confine yourself to just framing these needlepoint pictures. Though that is the most obvious idea, they lend themselves to other intriguing and practical uses. The circular Greek vase design, for instance, would make a handsome cover for a piano stool or footstool. Any of these completed needlepoints can be turned into cushions, tote bags, book covers, lingerie bags or what have you. A stouthearted needlepointer can produce a stunning rug by joining squares of the Matisse *Ivy in Flower*. You need not hesitate to *use* your finished needlepoint. The Paternayan Persian wool we recommend is exceedingly durable, and the colors grow mellow and lovelier with wear.

Supplies

Items one through five on this list are available wherever needlepoint supplies are sold. Items six through twelve can be purchased at art supply and/or stationery stores.

1. canvas
2. wool
3. needles
4. masking tape or bias tape
5. embroidery scissors

6. hard lead pencil, #4-H
7. a kneaded eraser
8. ruler
9. Sharpie felt-tip marker, black or brown
10. Liquitex acrylic paint
11. sable watercolor brush, #1
12. small tags on strings

THE CANVAS

Needlepoint canvas comes in single mesh, called mono, or double mesh, called penelope. Unless you have a personal preference for penelope, we recommend mono canvas for these projects; the holes are larger and easier to see than equivalent sizes in penelope canvas. Both styles come in a variety of gauges (threads per inch) and in widths from 36 to 60 inches. The best quality canvas has a smooth, hard finish and is evenly woven throughout. Be sure to inspect the piece for irregular threads or faulty mesh before you buy it.

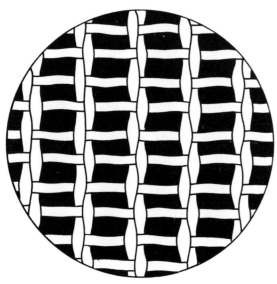

Penelope

Mono

THE WOOL

We recommend Paternayan Persian wool for these projects and the numbers in the color charts refer to that brand. This wool was originally imported for the repair of Oriental rugs, but embroiderers soon latched on to it because of its durability and sumptuous color range. It comes in strands of three threads, which can be separated into one- or two-ply or used intact as three-ply yarn, depending on the gauge of canvas you are using.

The exact amount of each color of wool depends upon the picture, its dimensions and the gauge of your canvas. It's best to rely on the judgment of an experienced salesperson for quantity. Select your colors by the numbers listed on the sample charts. Keep in mind that it's better to buy a little too much wool than to have the problem of matching dye-lots. However, if you do run short, refer to the instructions on matching wool in the section "Common Problems."

THE NEEDLES

Use only blunt-ended tapestry needles; the best ones come from England. Be sure your needle threads easily and slides through the mesh without tugging. Here are recommendations for threads of yarn and the correct needle size for the various gauges of canvas.

Canvas Gauge*	Threads of Persian Yarn	Needle
#18	one-ply	#22
#14	two-ply	#20
#10	three-ply (whole strand)	#18
#5	nine-ply (three strands)	"Quick Point" needle

OTHER NEEDLEWORK SUPPLIES

You'll need a pair of embroidery scissors with fine sharp points to clip ends accurately in tiny spaces. If you use a thimble, make sure it is smooth and doesn't snag the wool.

The raw edges of the canvas must be bound with bias

*All gauges are mono, except #5, which comes in double mesh only.

tape or masking tape to keep them from raveling. Bias tape may be stitched by hand or sewing machine. Use a zigzag stitch or sew several times around the canvas to hold the threads securely. One-inch-wide masking tape can be folded over the edges and pressed in place with a hard-edged tool.

For drawing the grid, you'll need a pencil, ruler, eraser, and either Liquitex acrylic paint and a brush or a waterproof felt-tip pen. The details of drawing and using the grid are explained further on.

You'll need tags to label each color of wool and mark it with a symbol that corresponds to the symbol on the graph.

How to Cut the Canvas

Your canvas must be cut to allow for seams, if any, and margins for convenience in handling. Each graph has information about the size of the finished work you get from each gauge of canvas. For instance, if the needlepoint picture runs 144 stitches across and 104 stitches down, on #10 gauge canvas you'd get a finished piece that measures approximately 14¼ by 9¾ inches. On a larger gauge canvas, such as #5, your picture would be about twice that size. If the equation of stitch-to-inch count seems a little off to you, it's because most canvases have a slight variation in the number of threads per inch running vertically and horizontally.

Hold your canvas so that the selvages are at the sides. (The selvage is the woven finished edge that runs the length of the bolt of canvas on each side.) Calculate your measurements as follows:

	Length	Width
Dimensions of graph	14¼ inches	9¾ inches
Seam allowance, if any, ¼ inch each side	½ inch	½ inch
Margin for handling, 2 inches each side	4 inches	4 inches
Size to cut canvas	18¾ inches	14¼ inches

If you plan to make a pillow or tote bag with a side wall, be sure to add the ¼-inch seam allowance to each side of the strip you cut for the insert. The back of the piece should naturally measure the same size as the front.

As soon as you've cut your canvas to the proper size, bind or tape the edges as described previously to prevent raveling.

How to Draw and Use the Grid

First of all, if you have never followed a graph before, don't panic. The graph is not a complicated mystery. The important thing to understand is how the stitch is represented. A stitch on the *canvas* is the wool that covers a pair of *intersecting* canvas threads. On the *graph,* it is represented by a symbol in a *square*. It's as simple as that.

Your canvas, when marked with its grid, will correspond stitch for stitch to the graph in the book. First, look at the graph of the picture you've chosen. You'll see that every tenth line is heavier than the others. Notice too that each graph is divided in half vertically and horizontally. This network of lines is called the grid.

stitches on canvas

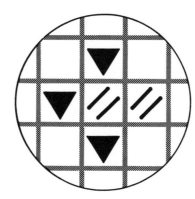

symbols on graph

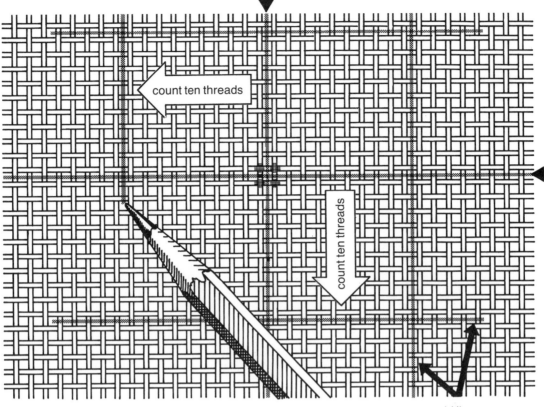

mark center

count ten threads

count ten threads

mark center

grid lines

To make a corresponding grid on your canvas, locate the vertical and horizontal center lines by measuring halfway in from the sides and halfway down between the top and bottom. With your #4-H pencil, draw these lines clear across the canvas, making them fall between two parallel threads. *Grid lines are always drawn between parallel threads of canvas.*

At the intersection of your two center lines, there are places for four stitches. With the pencil or acrylic paint, mark each of these canvas thread intersections; this will help you find the center of your work at a glance. Also mark the top of your canvas, remembering to keep the selvages at the sides. Next, working in either direction from the center, count ten canvas threads, and with your pencil, draw the first line of the grid. (Remember to draw *between* the parallel threads.) Count ten more canvas threads from this line and draw the next line. Continue counting groups of ten threads in both directions from the center until you have the same arrangement of grid lines on your canvas as there are accented lines on the graph in the book. The horizontal lines will intersect with the vertical lines to form little blocks of ten by ten canvas threads, or groups of 100 intersections to represent 100 stitches.

Next, count on the graph the number of spaces beyond the outermost accented lines. Mark them on your canvas and draw the outline around your grid. This is your outer margin.

Before proceeding further, check all your lines to be sure they correspond exactly to those in the book. If you have made a mistake, use your kneaded eraser and redraw the pencil lines. If all your pencil lines are correct, you should now mark them with a more visible permanent line. Use the Liquitex acrylic paint or felt-tip marker, but be absolutely certain the substance you use is waterproof. Don't rely on words like *waterproof* or *water-resistant*. Test even the brands we've recommended. Make a mark on a corner of your canvas. When it is thoroughly dry, scrub it with a damp cloth or brush. If any color runs, even the slightest, find another marker. You can't be too cautious about this because in blocking your canvas it must be quite saturated with water. If any color runs from the canvas into your wool, your needlepoint will be ruined. Don't be tempted to rely on a dark pencil for marking your grid, either; the lead or graphite will rub off and permanently discolor your wool.

Since the word *blocking* has been mentioned, this is the time to prepare for that step. Whether you intend to block the canvas yourself or take it to a professional, you must record the exact dimensions of your needlepoint *before* you start to work. Once you start the stitching, the canvas will tend to skew out of shape somewhat. On clean heavy paper, make an outline pattern of the correct dimensions of the canvas, including the taped edges. Set this pattern aside for later use.

The Stitches

Basically, the needlepoint stitch is a diagonal bit of wool that covers the intersection of two canvas threads (or two pairs of threads in the case of penelope canvas). The wool always comes from the lower left space to the upper right space. There are three ways of making this stitch. They all look the same on the front, but produce a different effect on the back and affect the quality of the needlepoint fabric differently. The stitches are called the *half-cross*, the *continental* and the *basketweave*. We will not consider the half-cross in this book because it doesn't combine well with the other stitches or give good coverage on mono canvas.

Beginners and even advanced needlepointers who want to refresh their memory should try the stitches on a small piece of canvas while reading the instructions.

THE CONTINENTAL STITCH

Start your stitch at the top right-hand corner of the area you wish to work. Bring the yarn from the back of the canvas, up through the lower left hole, Point #1 in the diagram. Take your yarn, on a diagonal, through the upper right-hand hole, Point #2, and in the same motion, pass the needle behind two vertical canvas threads at the back and up through the hole at Point #3. This is the beginning of the second stitch. Continue stitching this way until you reach the last stitch in the row. Complete this stitch, draw the needle to the back of the canvas, and then turn the canvas completely around, so that the bottom is now at the top, and you are working from right to left again. Pass the needle up through the hole at Point #9 and complete the row as before.

Continental

THE BASKETWEAVE STITCH

As in the continental stitch, you always start in the top right-hand corner of the area to be worked. But unlike the continental, the basketweave stitch is worked in diagonal rows rather than horizontal. And the canvas is never turned; it is always held in the same position. Bring the yarn from the back of the canvas to the front, through the hole at Point #1. Pass it diagonally to the upper right hole, Point #2, and in the same motion around the back and up through the hole at Point #3, across again to the upper right hole at Point #4, and in the same motion straight down, behind two horizontal canvas threads, and up through the hole at Point #5. Pass the needle to the diagonal upper right and into the hole at Point #6. As you follow this pattern, notice that you are working on a diagonal from a northwest direction to a southeast direction. On the return trip, the stitches travel from southeast to northwest. Notice, too, that the needle moves from stitch to stitch in a vertical position going down, and horizontally going up.

When you do basketweave, always stop work in the middle of a row with the needle in position for the next stitch. Otherwise, you may lose your place and work two rows in the same direction. If this happens, a ridge or permanent scar is created in the needlepoint fabric and it will not block out.

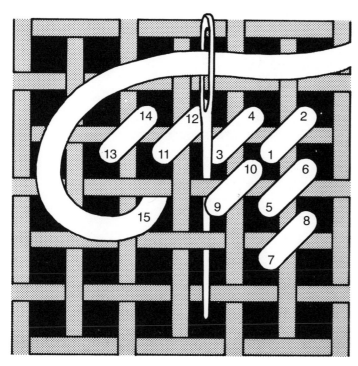

Basketweave

WHICH STITCH TO USE?

The continental stitch is used mostly for outlining or in small areas where only a few stitches of a color might appear. As you see from the diagram (Fig. 1), the continental stitch pulls both the front and back yarn strongly in the same direction. If used throughout the canvas, the completed fabric skews off in one direction and is difficult to block into shape. The basketweave stitch, on the other hand, is recommended for all major design areas and the background. In this stitch, the tension is distributed in two opposite directions (Fig. 2) and the canvas remains relatively stable. The basketweave stitch also makes for very solid coverage on the back and nice plump stitches on the front.

Fig. 1   Continental

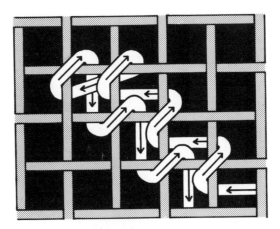

Fig. 2   Basketweave

How to Work from the Graph

The needlepoint graph is a map that plots the location of each stitch in the needlepoint fabric. Each graph is divided by the grid into blocks of 100 stitches — ten spaces across and ten spaces down. Your canvas, with its grid, is also divided this way. It is therefore possible for you to locate any stitch on the graph and the corresponding stitch on your canvas by counting from the lines of the grid. You never have to count more than ten stitches in any direction.

The colors are represented by symbols, and each square contains one such symbol. A blank square is also a symbol and is usually used to represent the background color. Tie a little tag around each hank of wool, labeling it with its color chart number and symbol before you start to work.

There is actually only one graph for each picture, but it is presented in several sections for your convenience. First, you see the whole graph, reduced to fit on one page. You can't work from this small size, but you'll get an overall idea of how the separate sections relate to the whole.

The next graph is a detail of the middle section, showing the placement of the first colors to be worked into the canvas. They have been isolated to make the first counting of stitches easier for you.

The next series of graphs are sections of the master graph, divided down the center lines. They appear in sequence beginning with the top half, from left to right. Each section is keyed by letter to the master graph.

Eventually, everyone finds a method of working that is personally satisfying. But generally, it's a good idea to start with the center graph and place one or two colors correctly. You can then count from these stitches or from the nearest grid lines for the placement of your next stitches. It's best to fill in the areas closest to the center lines and work in a pattern that fans out toward the edges. You might find it simpler to work a part of the picture that is a complete unit in itself, such as a leaf or animal form, without regard for the methodical outward progression. Follow whatever plan suits you best, but keep a constant check on the accuracy of your color placement.

You may find it convenient to have the graphs enlarged photostatically so you can carry your work about without carrying the whole book. Some people find symbols a strain to deal with and prefer to color sections of the graphs with light-colored pencils or felt-tip markers. Another helpful device can be made by cutting a little window, the size of one grid square, out of a piece of lightweight cardboard. You can fix this opening over the square you wish to isolate on the graph. Secure the cardboard with masking tape, and when that area is completed, gently peel back the tape and move your template to the next block.

Common Problems and Some Solutions

HOW TO START AND END A PIECE OF YARN

Never use knots. Pull the yarn through the canvas, allowing a 1-inch tail to remain at the back. Hold this tail in position so that your first four or five stitches cover it and anchor it in place. Clip the remaining end immediately. Work your yarn to within 2 inches of its end. Pull it through to the back, weave it through four or five stitches *away* from the direction of your work, then backtrack and weave it toward your last stitch. Clip the end.

HOW TO AVOID LUMPS

Lumpy sections are caused by improper handling of ends and runners. A runner is a length of wool at the back of the canvas that spans two separate areas of the same color (Fig. 1). If you must use a runner, do not let it get tangled in the stitching. As soon as possible, work another color nearby,

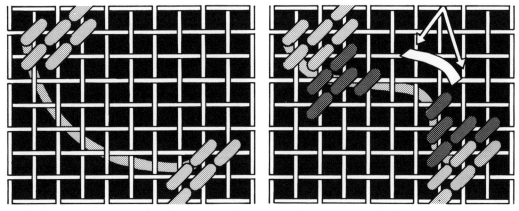

Fig. 1   a runner   Fig. 2.

anchor the ends of the runner in the adjacent colors and clip away the entire center, as shown in Figure 2. Always anchor ends and tails of wool in sections that have accumulated the least bulk and trim the excess immediately to avoid tangles.

HOW TO KEEP YOUR WORK CLEAN

If a strand of wool gets dirty, it will create a line or spot of dirt in your needlepoint that will be difficult to remove. Always wash your hands before starting work and during extended periods of work. It's also a good idea to keep your wool in a clear plastic bag. Your canvas, too, should be protected in a bag or wrapped in a clean towel between working sessions.

HOW TO HANDLE SKIPPED STITCHES AND MISTAKES

A skipped stitch is not a serious problem. When you hold your completed canvas up to the light, a skipped stitch will show up as a pinpoint of light. Use straight pins to mark these spaces, and then fill them with the appropriate color. Be sure to bury the ends of your wool securely in uncongested areas at the back.

It is a bit more complicated to correct a mistake after the canvas is completed, but don't hesitate to do so if it's a serious error. Carefully cut the stitches at the back, without damaging the canvas threads. Rip away enough stitching, even if you have to intrude into healthy areas, so that you have ends that are long enough to anchor to the fabric. Rework the area and make sure you secure all loose ends.

HOW TO MATCH YARN

If you run short of a color, it's best not to rely on dye-lot numbers for matching, as there are variations in color from batch to batch. In a busy portion of the canvas, an exact match is not essential. But for background color or large, uninterrupted areas of one color, an exact match is essential. Take a piece of the original yarn and a hank of the new wool into bright sunlight. Hold them both in the same direction, and you'll get a pretty good idea of the color match.

Blocking

Some people can work the most complicated needlepoint designs but throw up their hands at the idea of blocking their own work. Blocking is not at all difficult, and the projects in this book are simple shapes that should give you no trouble.

First, if you have bound your canvas with masking tape, you'll have to rebind it with bias tape or turn under a narrow hem of canvas (about ¼ to ½ inch). Masking tape will not survive the wetting process required for blocking. The reason you don't turn a hem on the canvas in the first place is that the wool would catch on the rough edges, and your hands, too, would take a beating from the stiff scratchy edges of the canvas.

Next, find a board of the right size. Plywood, which is warp-proof, or an old drawing board works very well. Find the paper pattern you made of the original size of your needlepoint and staple it to the board. If you have removed masking tape and turned a hem on the canvas, reduce the dimensions by the depth of the hem. With a pencil, mark the midpoint of each side of the pattern.

You are now ready for the wetting-down process. Turn

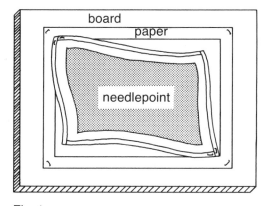

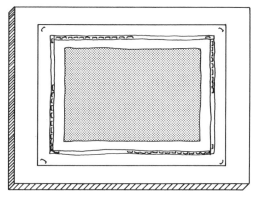

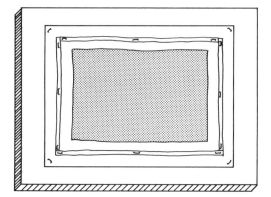

Fig. 1

Fig. 3

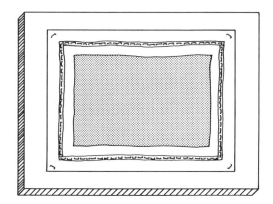

Fig. 2

Fig. 4

your needlepoint facedown on a clean towel near the sink. With a sponge or wad of clean cloth, liberally dampen the back with cool water. Do not soak it under the faucet, but be sure it is thoroughly saturated. You'll notice that the entire canvas will go limp. Don't worry. It means the sizing has dissolved so you can maneuver the canvas back to its original shape. The natural body of the canvas will return when it dries.

Carefully move your needlepoint to the board you've prepared. Lay the work, facedown, on the paper pattern and start matching the canvas to the outline. Fix the corners in place first. Use a staple gun with stainless steel staples. Proceed from one corner to the next. By the time you reach the fourth corner, you may have to tug a bit. Don't be timid; the canvas can take it.

Next, move to the midpoint of your canvas along any edge and staple it to the midpoint of the paper pattern. Do this

on all four sides. You now have four corners and four mid-
points fastened in place.

From here on, choose any midpoint and work away from
it toward the corner, stapling through the binding or hem.
Staple at close intervals so there is no sag. When you've
finished half of one side, move to the half diagonally opposite. Start at the midpoint and staple away toward the corner. Move to a third side; complete half the tacking from
the midpoint out, and then move to the opposite side and
work toward the diagonally opposite corner. When you
have completed half of each of the four sides, return to the
first side and complete the stapling to the other corner. Follow the procedure used in the first round, alternating areas
of tacking to distribute the tension evenly.

Leave the board and canvas to dry in a well-ventilated
place, away from radiators or artificial heat. It should dry
slowly. You may have to wait two days or more before you
can remove the canvas from the board. When you do, you'll
be thrilled to see how loose stitches have evened up, and
how finished and professional your needlepoint looks.

If the sides are straight and the corners nice and square,
you can improve your canvas further by holding a steam
iron just above the front surface of the work. Never let the
iron touch the wool, but allow the steam to flow through the
fabric and plump up the stitches that have flattened out in
the blocking process.

If by some chance, and it does happen, the first blocking
doesn't completely straighten out the shape of your canvas,
you may repeat the procedure without damaging the needlepoint. But again, we encourage you to do what suits you
best. If you are timid about blocking your own needlepoint, your supply store, framer or upholsterer is prepared
to handle the job — and you can get to work on your next
masterpiece.

THE PAINTINGS
AND
GRAPHS

An Egyptian Wall Painting

If there was one single force that dominated the lives of the ancient Egyptians, it was their religion and its concern with life after death. Not that they spent their days in morbid contemplation. They lived full, productive lives. They were prolific and exquisite craftsmen in all the arts: glass-making, goldsmithing, stoneware, jewelry, weaving, as well as dance and music. Their contributions in architecture, astronomy and mathematics are staggering.

But their religion prepared them for death as a continuation of life. Those who could afford it took great pains to build secure tombs, which they filled with food, utensils and all their prized possessions to insure a happy, cozy hereafter. It was on the walls of these tombs that much of Egyptian painting was discovered. For in addition to the actual food and vital supplies buried in the tombs, the walls were filled with pictures of all such creature comforts. If supplies ran out, a few words from the deceased to a god of the dead would transform a picture into the real thing, thus assuring the deceased an endless supply.

The walls of the tombs were also adorned with pictures of seasonal activities such as planting, harvesting, fishing, weaving, feasting, dancing and religious rites. These pictures were, in a sense, a calendar of the year's events and were intended to enable the deceased to continue to participate in the pleasures of his lifetime.

The art in the tombs was essentially an art of drawing. Figures and objects were drawn or incised in fine elegant lines and enhanced with brilliant color. The human figure was consistently drawn with head, arms and legs in profile, shoulders and torso in three-quarter view, and the eye in full view. Though the artists were surely skillful enough to render more naturalistic images, they made no attempt to do so. They were not interested in naturalism. Their flat stylized drawings of the human form were austere, dignified symbols and apparently conveyed an image more meaningful than false illusions of reality.

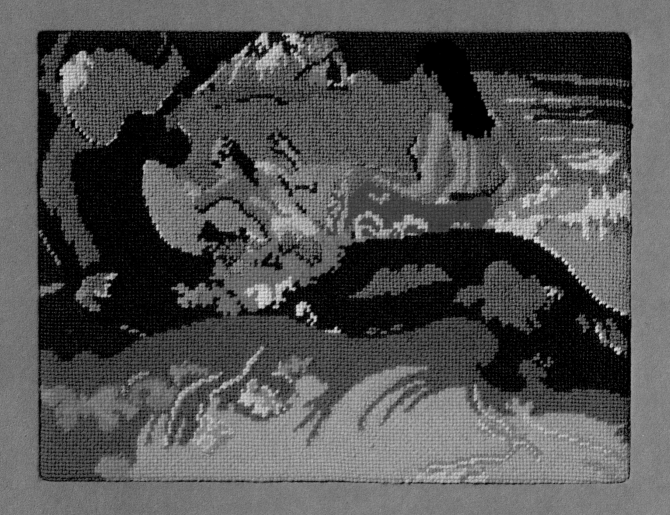

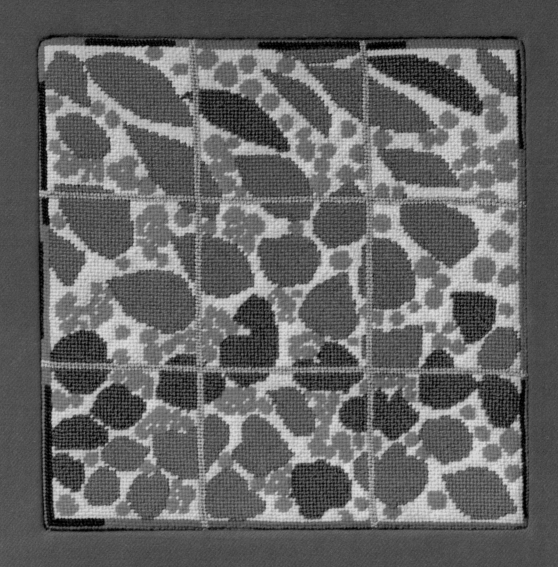

Although the pharaohs and men of means commissioned the great tombs, men and women of all ranks, as well as gods and kings, were represented in the decorations. Gods were made to look like humans. The human soul was represented by a bird — sometimes a bird with the head of a man. Animals such as the bull, the cat and the crocodile were considered sacred and appear frequently in paintings, sculpture and pottery decorations.

In this needlepoint adaptation, the architect Ankerkhau is shown worshiping the bennu. The original wall painting was found in the tomb of Ankerkhau in Thebes. It dates back to circa 1190 B.C. The legend of the bennu corresponds to the legend of the phoenix. This mythic bird supposedly lives for hundreds of years, dies on a funeral pyre and rises again from its own ashes to start life anew. The ancient Egyptians worshiped the bennu as part of their sun worship rites. They saw a parallel between the life cycle of the bennu and the sun's daily cycle. The sun, too, dies in its own flames each evening and emerges again each morning. The bird, like the sun, was a symbol of immortality.

The needlepoint sample was worked by Marge Gross.

Thread Count: 144 x 163

Canvas Gauge	Approximate Size
#18	8⅛ inches × 8⅞ inches
#14	10¼ inches × 11½ inches
#10	14⅛ inches × 15½ inches
# 5	28⅜ inches × 32⅝ inches

A B

C D

Pale orange #464 — ▨ #389 Gray

Red orange #280 • ▧ #005 White

Red #210 ✕ ■ #108 Black

Lavender #743 ╲ ☐ #425 Orange

Note: This graph is so easy, we've shown only the symbols that *outline* the shapes instead of repeating all the symbols in the center graph.

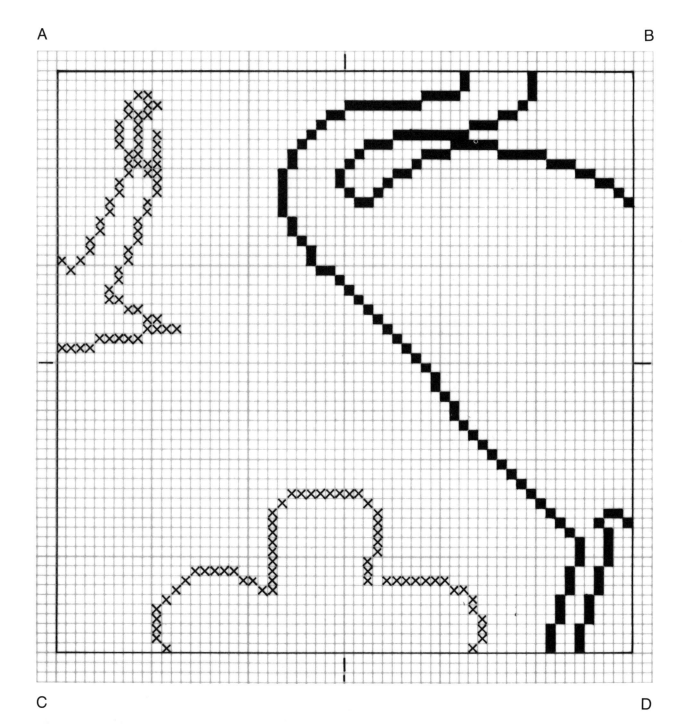

A

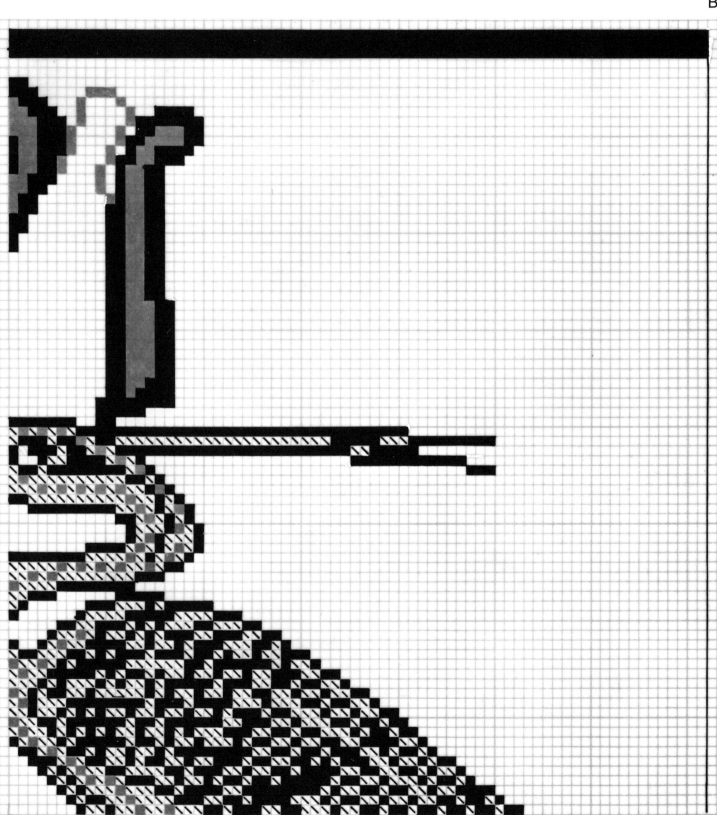

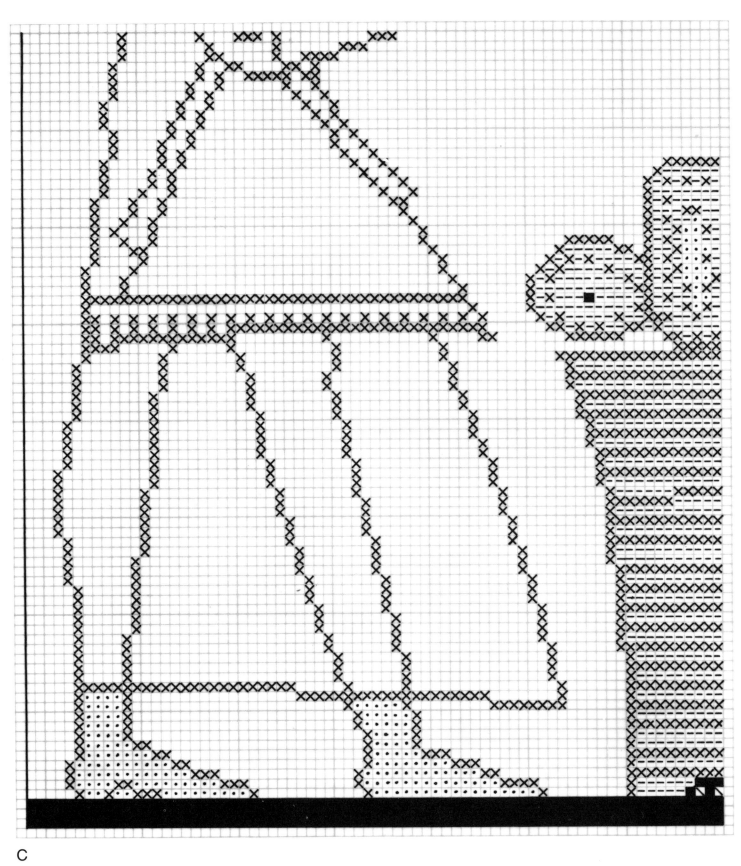

C

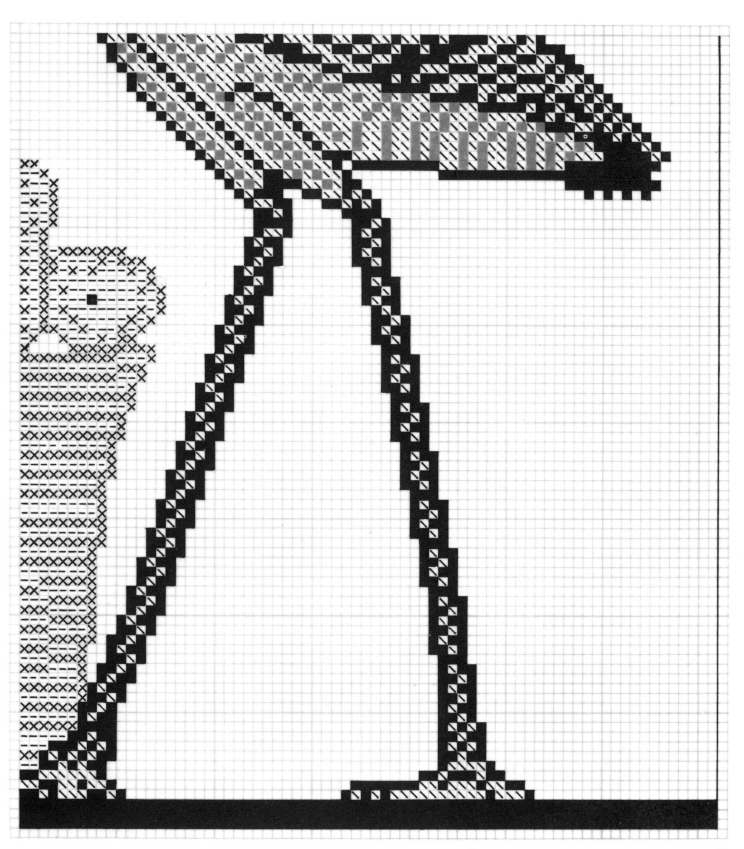

A Greek Vase Painting

All ancient people made "pots" — to drink from, to hold water, oil, wine and also to store the remains of their dead. But artistically speaking, Greek vases are in a class by themselves. They are esteemed for the unique harmony that was achieved between the form of the vase and the painting on it. Some historians maintain that the Greeks reached such heights because of the fierce competitive nature of their society. Each artist worked feverishly to outdo his predecessors and his contemporaries. They so jealously guarded their artistic reputations that both the potter and the painter signed their names to each piece. If a potter was also a skilled painter, and vice versa, he would sign the vase twice!

Vase making was the major art form in Greece for a thousand years, starting in about 1100 B.C. That was long before they tried their hands at sculpture and architecture. The earliest vase paintings were, like all primitive decorations, flat, geometric and abstract. But as the Greeks expanded geographically, they were influenced by older Eastern and Oriental cultures. Between the eighth and sixth centuries B.C., fantastic plant and animal forms appeared, and finally very expressive and intricate paintings of human figures. These late vases are like pages of a history book for the information they reveal about Greek life — their dress, their religion, their cultural and social activities, their gods, myths and military expeditions.

Two basic painting techniques were used: black-figure and red-figure design. In the black-figure technique, the figures and pattern were painted in black silhouette on the red clay ground. In red-figure pottery, the figures were "reserved" in the natural red color of the pot, and the background was painted out in black. Thin sensitive lines were added to depict drapery, body contours and other details. Frequently, both black- and red-figure techniques were combined in one pot.

The design for this needlepoint is adapted from the interior of a 4½-inch black-figured drinking cup called a kylix.* It was created in 540 B.C. by Exekias, one of the most famous potter-painters of his time. The original cup is in the Staatliche Antikensammlungen, Munich.

The picture relates a myth about Dionysus, the god of wine. It seems Dionysus was once kidnapped by a band of pirates, but while on the high seas, he invoked his godly powers and caused grapevines to grow in profusion all over the ship. They tangled in the sails, fouled the gear and generally confounded his captors. In terror and alarm, the kidnappers jumped overboard and were immediately turned into dolphins. In the painting, Dionysus is pictured returning home in triumph, accompanied by seven dolphins and seven bunches of grapes for good luck. (A likely story.)

The needlepoint sample was worked by Elaine Ormond.

Thread Count: 144 × 148

Canvas Gauge	Approximate Size
#18	8⅛ inches × 8 inches
#14	10¼ inches × 10½ inches
#10	14⅛ inches × 14 inches
# 5	28⅜ inches × 29⅝ inches

*Greek pots are referred to by various names depending on their form and use. Here are a few words to round out your Greek vocabulary and help with your crossword puzzles: kylix . . . a drinking cup, krater . . . a mixing bowl, hydria . . . a two- or three-handled jug for water, amphora . . . a two-handled vessel for storing wine, oil or other liquids.

A

B

C

D

Purplish brown #115 ■   ▨ #005 White

Mauve #893 ✕   ☐ #225 Coral

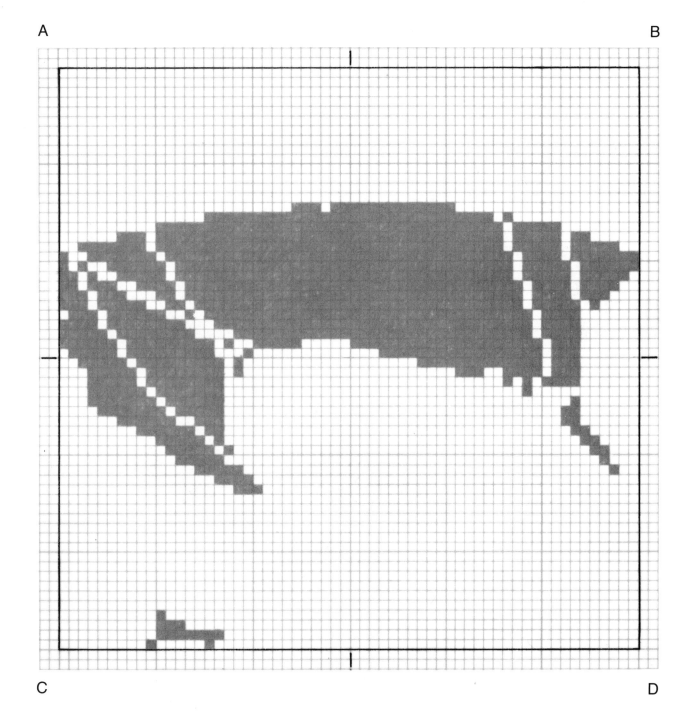

A   B

C   D

A

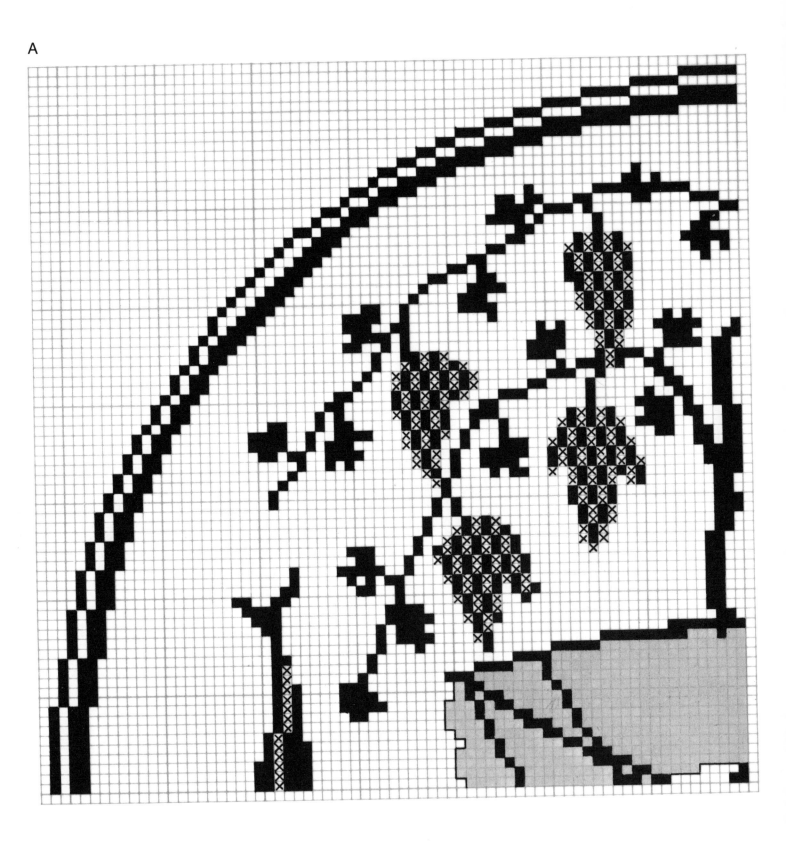

B

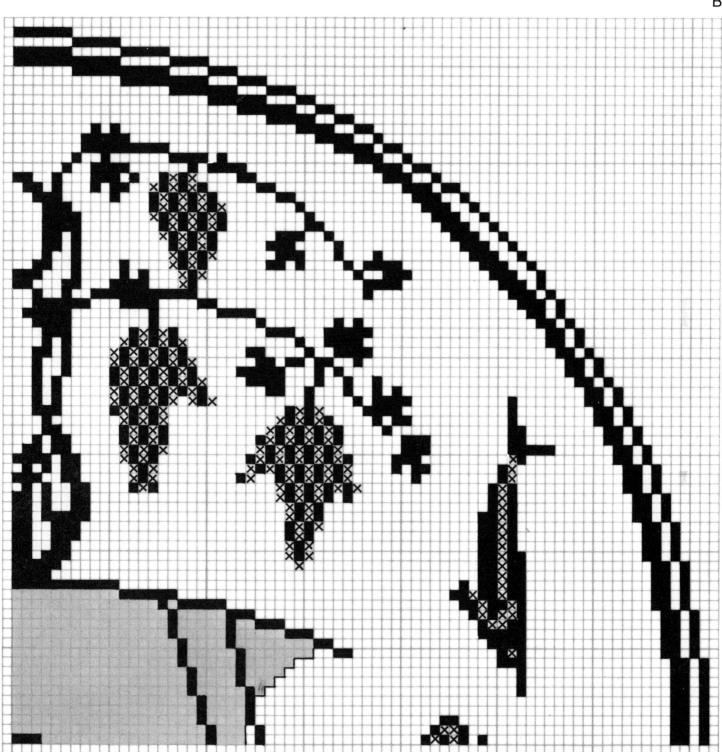

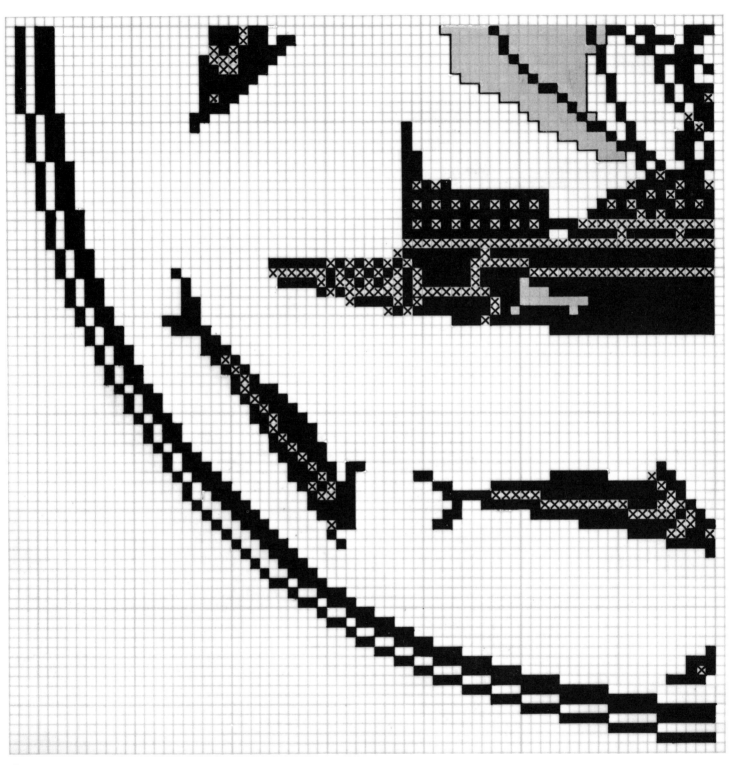

C

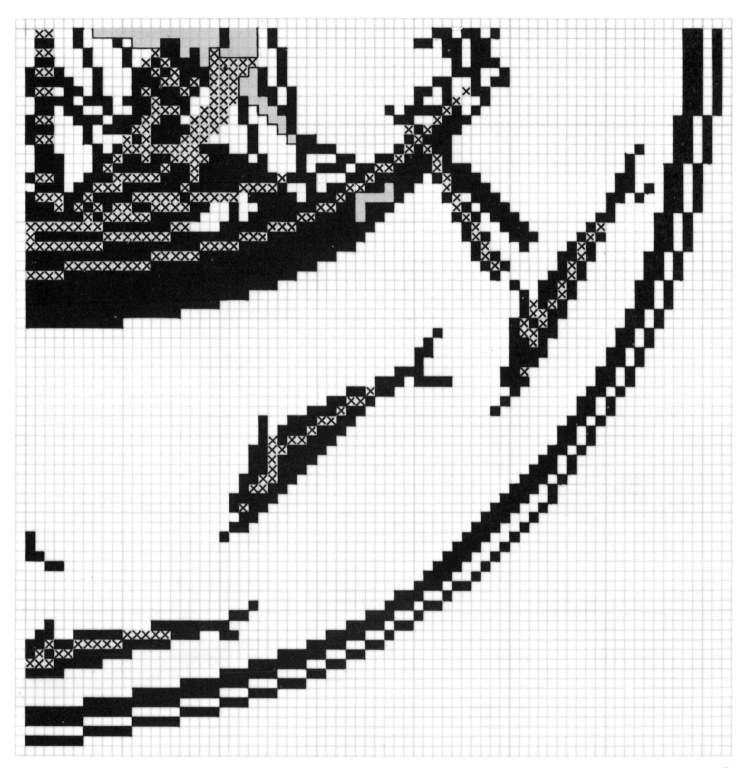

D

An Illumination

The Shepherd David

In Medieval Europe, all art was religious in nature — for two very strong reasons. The two main patrons of the arts were the Church and the kings who claimed that their right to rule came directly from God. It was deemed that faithfulness to God went hand-in-hand with faithfulness to one's rulers. To insure their power, these temporal and secular rulers inundated their subjects with compelling reminders of their religious obligations. Courts and cathedrals, alike, were resplendent with dazzling statuary, stained glass, tapestries, carvings, textiles and art objects — all devoted to religious themes: the holy family, the saints, religious symbols and illustrations of acts of faith. There were no notable attempts at change or innovation; the same images were repeated over and over again so that everyone would understand the message.

In the monasteries, the monks, who were the chief disseminators of religious teaching, developed yet another religious art form — and a most exquisite one — the illuminated manuscript. With only the Scriptures as their text, they reproduced and decorated manuscripts and bound them into separate volumes. They produced Bibles, Old and New Testaments, Psalters (books containing the Book of Psalms), Missals, Sacramentaries (used in the Mass) and other liturgical texts. The craftsmanship and materials were unsurpassed, but never for the sake of artistry — only for the glory of God.

The books were lettered in ornamental script on vellum (calfskin) or parchment (sheepskin). Manuscripts commissioned by royalty or wealthy patrons were luxuriously bound in fine leather, embellished with gold and encrusted with precious gems.

In the earliest manuscripts, the main focus of attention was the calligraphy, or lettering. In some cases, highly ornamental borders were added. Later, they took to enlarging and enhancing the initial letter of each page, transforming it into an animal form, a human face or other decorative element. In time, small spot illustrations were sprinkled through the text and in the margins of the pages. Finally, the form evolved to include full-page illustrations and heavily decorated title pages. Throughout, the manuscripts were painted in brilliant hand-ground colors and often embellished with gold or silver. The brilliance and glow of these pages explain the name "illumination."

Although the monks were expert craftsmen in their specialties as calligraphers, illuminators or binders, they made no stylistic innovations. They worked in the manner of the prevailing art form. Depth, perspective, illusions of reality were ignored. They represented roundness of form by contours of drapery rather than by modeling the figure. Spatial relations were indicated by placing close figures in the lower section of the picture and distant figures higher up on the vertical plane. These were the concepts that prevailed in the stained-glass windows and panel paintings of the period and, what is especially interesting, were rediscovered and adopted by modern masters in the late nineteenth century in Europe.

This needlepoint adaptation is based on an illustration, *The Shepherd David,* in an illuminated Old Testament manuscript produced in France, circa 1250. The original manuscript is in the Pierpont Morgan Library in New York City, whose collection of rare books is among the finest in the world.

The needlepoint sample was worked by Ina Zoob.

Thread Count: 139 × 169

Canvas Gauge	Approximate Size
#18	7⅞ inches × 9¼ inches
#14	9⅞ inches × 12 inches
#10	12⅜ inches × 16 inches
# 5	27⅜ inches × 33¾ inches

A B

C D

Yellow #457 \

Blue #773 /

Light green #570 ▨

Sienna #414 —

Light sienna #426 ▨

■ #110 *Dark brown*

○ #380 *Dark blue*

✕ #530 *Green*

☐ #005 *White*

A B

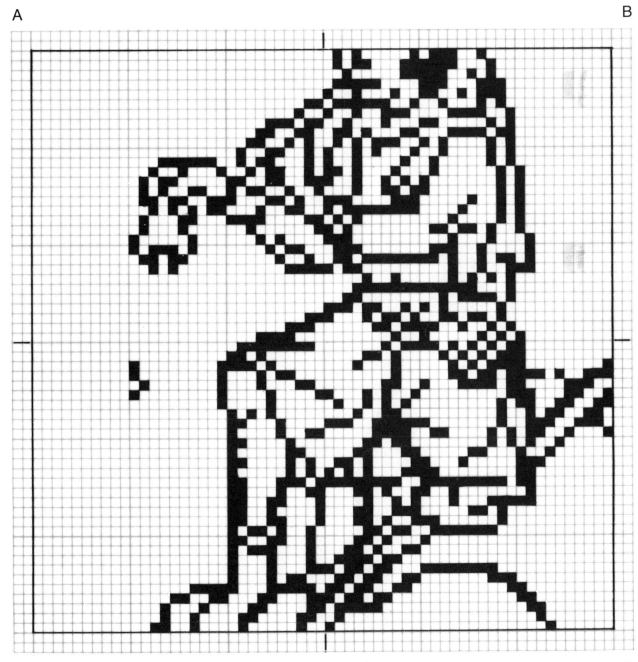

C D

A

B

An Islamic Miniature

Prince Riding an Elephant

It is a curious fact that while early Western art was totally involved with religious themes and images, Islamic law (Mohammedanism) strictly forbade the depiction and worship of images. This restriction was a most powerful influence and gave Islamic art its unique character.

The Islamic world, which included the Mohammedan peoples of Spain, North Africa, the Arabic countries, Turkey, Persia and India, created an art form based almost completely on calligraphy. Since it was the calligrapher who produced the Koran, the holy book, it was he who enhanced the word of God. The calligrapher was esteemed above all other artists, and the people developed a taste for the cursive, arabesque forms of his script as a decorative motif. While human images were prohibited, animal, plant and geometric forms were interwoven with calligraphic form in intricate endless patterns. These themes appeared everywhere — in pottery, metalware, architecture, weavings, glass and textiles.

But the desire to reproduce the human figure could not be entirely suppressed. Representations of the human form did finally appear, but never in religious objects or buildings directly connected with religious activity. While each of the Moslem countries developed its own characteristic style, successive invasions of Mongol tribes from the north caused vast migrations and fusions of ideas. The mingling of all the exotically decorative styles culminated in the exquisite Persian miniatures of the sixteenth century. These paintings, for the most part, were commissioned by princes of enormous wealth and unabashed appetites for beauty. The small paintings were book illustrations — exotic in color, opulent in materials and designed for pure visual delight. There was no attempt at naturalism or illusion. They introduced the high horizon line, and tilted the foreground into a vertical plane so that many figures could be shown in a small space. Scenery was treated like stage flats. No decorative detail of leaves, birds, flowers or fabric patterns was omitted. The purpose of these miniature gems was to delight the eye and soul, and even scenes of war and violence were treated with poetic grace.

Miniature paintings produced in India are closely related to the earlier Persian models. In fact, two eminent Persian masters were imported into India to set up a school to teach the craft. But during the early Mughal (Mongol) rule in India, a fusion of Hindu and Moslem cultures was encouraged. Visitors from the West also brought new ideas. The amalgam of all these influences resulted in a style that was more naturalistic — not so purely decorative. Indian miniatures of the period showed more concern with human and animal forms. Our needlepoint adaptation of *Prince Riding an Elephant* is typical. Indian artists progressed, too, in their attempts at portraiture and studies of scenic and architectural details. While not as intricate as the Persian, the Indian miniatures have a clarity and depth of color that is breathtaking.

The original painting *Prince Riding an Elephant* is Indian, of the Mughal School, and dates back to the late sixteenth–early seventeenth century. It is in the collection of the Metropolitan Museum of Art, New York City.

The needlepoint sample was worked by Betty McDonnell.

Thread Count: 171 × 129

Canvas Gauge	Approximate Size
#18	9⅝ inches × 7 inches
#14	12⅛ inches × 9⅛ inches
#10	16¾ inches × 12⅛ inches
# 5	33¾ inches × 25¾ inches

Medium green #527 ∽ || #287 Pink
Dark green #505 ◣   ⊙ #653 Fuschia
Yellow #437 ○   = #255 Medium pink
or Gold metallic thread #521 ✕   — #420 Light sienna
Red #958 ●   ▨ #172 Sienna
Light gray #164 ╱   ▨ #750 Dark teal
Medium gray #162 | • #005 White
Darkest gray #108 ■   ☐ #466 Camel

A   B

C   D

A

B

C

A Japanese Screen

Cranes by Sakai Hoitsu (1761–1828)

When we think of Japanese art, we invariably think of the popular Japanese woodcuts of the nineteenth century, which were remarkable not only in themselves, but for the tremendous influence they had on modern European painting. But the history of Japanese painting goes much farther back — to the sixth century, when Buddhism was first introduced from China. At that time, and for hundreds of years afterward, Japanese culture followed the Chinese closely in all things — especially religion, art and architecture. Japanese temples, shrines, wall paintings and decorations were indistinguishable from the Chinese.

The first truly original Japanese style appeared in the early twelfth century. With the rise of a wealthy ruling class to sponsor young artists, the Japanese broke free from the constrained elegance of the Chinese style. The Japanese were a more aggressive, more vigorous people, and their art form reflected this character. Their drawing was more animated, their color more sumptuous and their passion for decoration uninhibited. They also broke from the confinement of purely religious themes. They produced scroll paintings with exquisitely rendered scenes of heroic Japanese legends and elaborate court life. This period — the twelfth to fourteenth century — was a golden age of Japanese art.

In the fourteenth century, from China again, came a new religious influence — Zen Buddhism — and a new art form. This contemplative, austere religion deplored the material excesses of the established religion. In art, color was abandoned for India ink pictures rendered in a range of purely gray tones. Brush strokes were pared down to essentials. Instead of panoramic landscapes, a picture was a terse poetic image — a single object — painted, not to imitate nature, but to evoke a spiritual unity with it.

This austere India ink style, known as *Sumi-e,* could not contain the Japanese spirit forever. In the late sixteenth century, it burst forth in another era of opulence. Artists combined their elegant India ink brushwork with brilliant Japanese color. They silver- and gold-leafed screens, and painted over them with ink and lavish color. Our needle-point adaptation of a screen painting is typical of the splendor of the era. The revival of the Japanese style was nurtured by the wealthy and expansive Tokugawa dynasty. For three hundred years, from 1603 to 1868, it reigned in peace, prosperity and isolation, taking pleasure in daily life and commissioning works of art that reflected this spirit.

Cranes by Sakai Hoitsu (1761–1828), the screen painting from which our needlepoint was adapted, is typical of the Tokugawa era. The original screen is in the Worcester Art Museum, Worcester, Massachusetts, a contribution from the Charlotte E. W. Buffington Fund.

The needlepoint sample was worked by Beka Martin.

Thread Count: 140 × 147

Canvas Gauge   Approximate Size
- #18   7⅞ inches × 8 inches
- #14   9⅞ inches × 10½ inches
- #10   13¾ inches × 14 inches
- # 5   27⅝ inches × 29½ inches

A   B

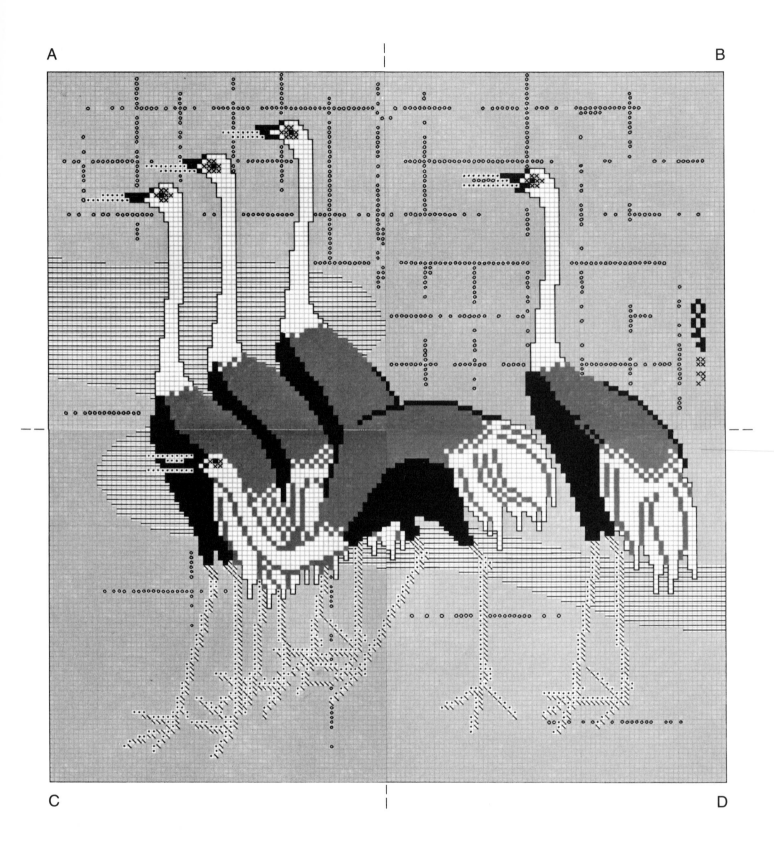

C   D

Dark blue #308 —   \ #414 Brick red

Pale gold #492 •   ╳ #242 Red

Gold #433 ▨   ○ #145 Dark gold

Dark gray #108 ■   □ #005 White

Lavender gray #184 ▩

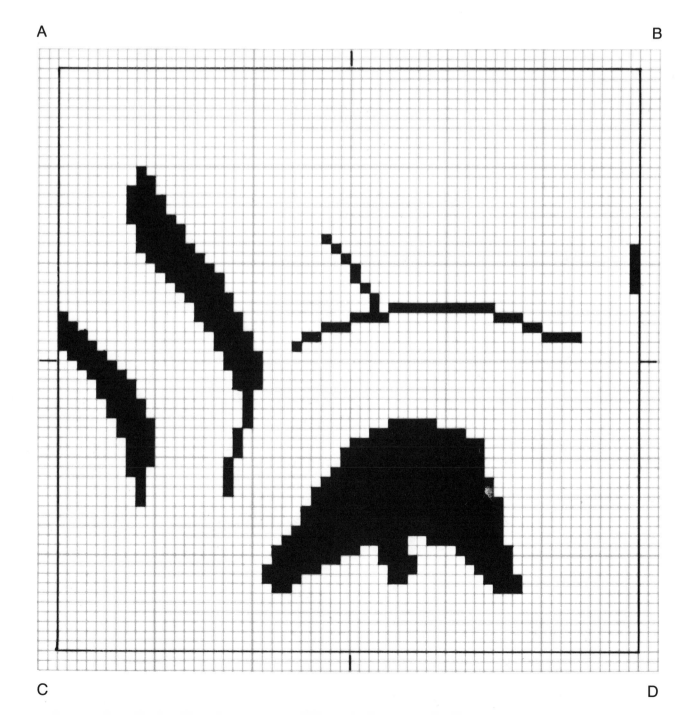

A

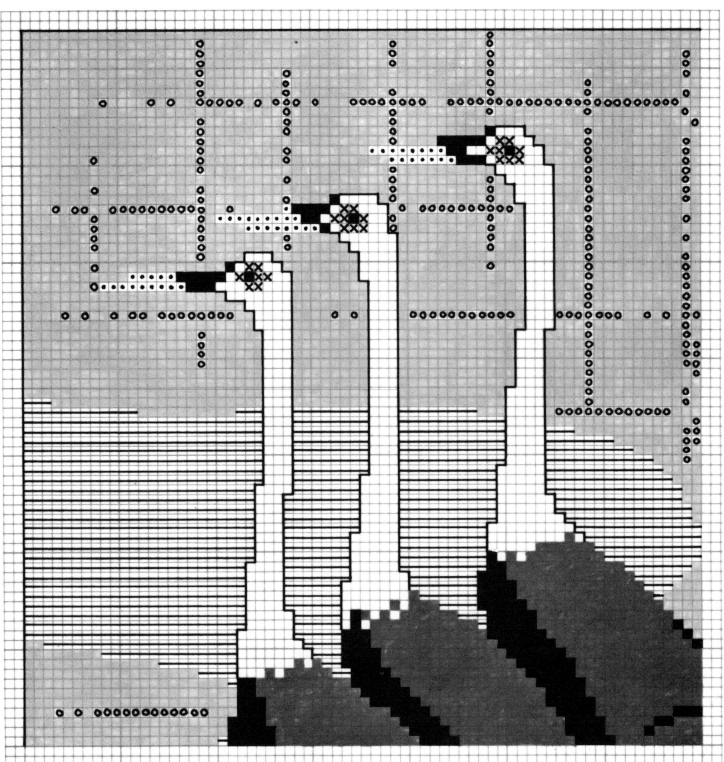

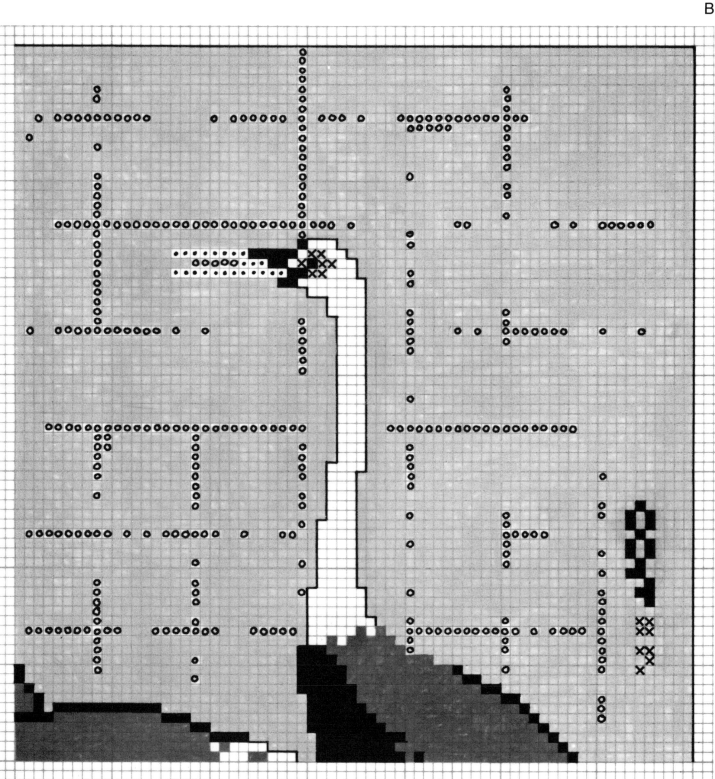

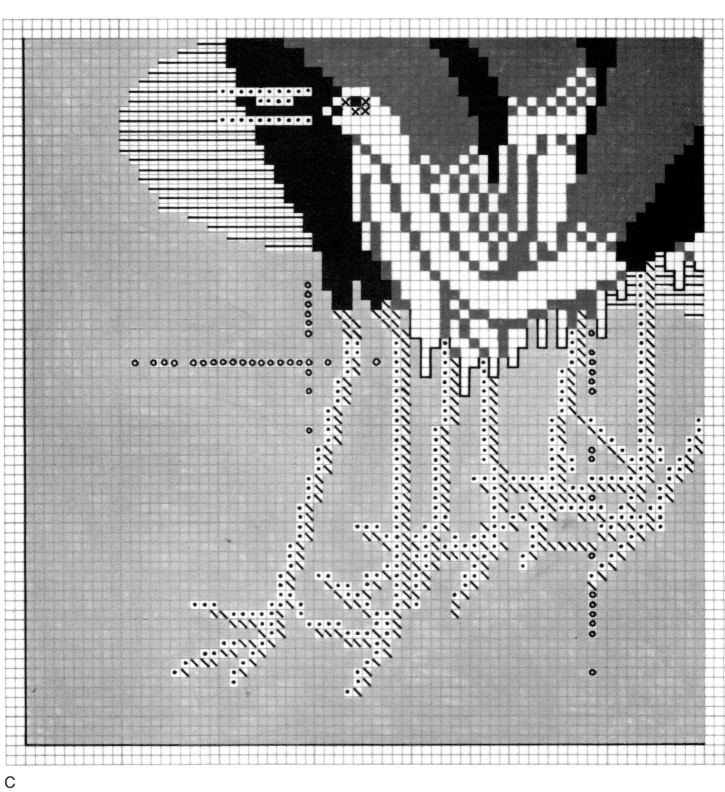

C

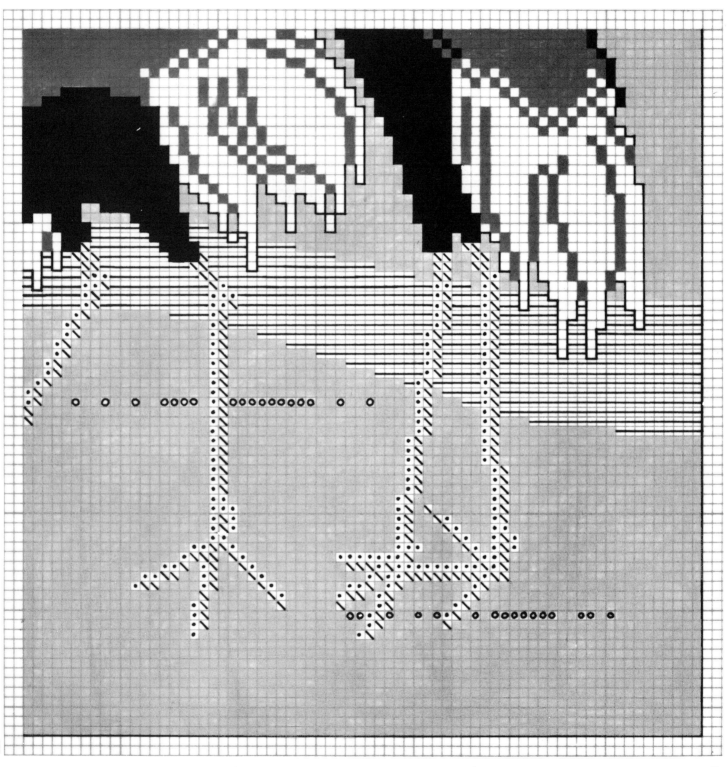

D

An American School Painting

Flowers and Fruit, Anonymous (mid-nineteenth century)

If you examine any collection of early American art, you'll surely be struck by the number of works that are labeled "Anonymous." This doesn't mean that our art historians are poor detectives, but it does give us some clue about the nature of art in the early years of the American republic.

To start with, the first settlers who came to carve a livable world out of the wilderness had to be rugged, skilled artisans — not gentleman artists! Once settled in their new communities, the morally rigid Puritans still held a dim view of art and decoration for its own sake. If their souls cried out for a bit of beauty, they tolerated it in useful objects only. Since there were no trained artists to fulfill even their meager needs, every skilled craftsman expanded his horizons. A house painter, who knew his way about with paints and brushes, also took to painting signs, decorating coaches, painting firescreens and rug patterns on bare floors. (Rugs were expensive and hard to come by.) In the Pennsylvania Dutch settlements, blacksmiths not only shod horses and made firearms and farm implements, they also designed weather vanes, decorative hinges, latches and doorknobs. And every colonial woman who made a quilt for her bed or embroidered a sampler for her wall was an artist in her own right.

By the middle of the eighteenth century, settlements grew into cities. A growing middle-class population started to reach out for some of the niceties of sophisticated European society. They wanted paintings for their homes, and skilled craftsmen who could paint portraits or scenic views were much in demand. Some successful painters gave up their original craft to study fine art. Men like the famous Benjamin West and John Singleton Copley went abroad to study and refine their skills. In larger cities, academies were established to train young ladies in the art of drawing, stenciling, painting on cloth and other crafts deemed natural to the "feminine nature."

But in the hinterlands, the very democratic nature of American art was still in evidence. The countryside was swarming with self-taught artists. With panels on their backs, colors and brushes in their saddlebags, they went from door to door, peddling their art for a night's lodging and a few meals. They offered to paint portraits (individuals or family groups), stencil floors, decorate chairs, screens, clocks or what have you. A familiar and favorite theme, sometimes executed on a panel or on cloth, was a flowers-and-fruit arrangement. It not only appealed to the earthy settlers' sense of the good and wholesome, but was, in a sense, a glorification of God's bounty.

It was these self-taught, "anonymous" artists — untrained in European painterly mannerisms — who painted with a clear eye and painstaking devotion to their task that produced a style of art that was honest, un-self-conscious and uniquely American.

This needlepoint design was adapted from an American painting by an anonymous artist of the mid-nineteenth century. The original is in the collection of the National Gallery of Art, Washington, D.C., a gift of Edgar William and Bernice Chrysler Garbisch.

The needlepoint sample was worked by Brande Ormond.

Thread Count: 134 × 174

Canvas Gauge	Approximate Size
#18	7½ inches × 9½ inches
#14	9½ inches × 12⅜ inches
#10	13⅛ inches × 16½ inches
# 5	26⅜ inches × 34⅞ inches

A   B

C   D

Pale yellow #455 •
Yellow #457 —
Pale green #592 //
Light green #589 /
Medium green #534 ■
Aqua #G32 ●
Orange #978 ∽
Red #843 ✕
Light olive #590 =
Medium olive #555 ⊙

⋰ #367 Dark teal
\ #B43 Pale blue
░ #743 Light blue
◢ #741 Medium blue
∪ #312 Dark blue
| #194 Light sienna
+ #248 Medium sienna
■ #247 Dark sienna
○ #005 White
□ #108 Darkest gray
Z #271 Pink

A   B

C   D

A

C

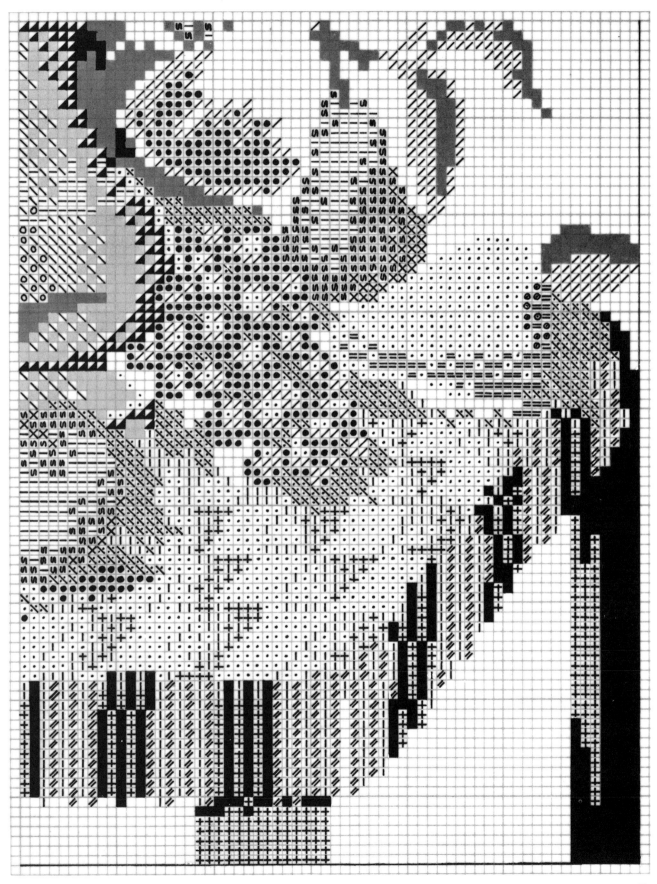

D

Fatata Te Miti

by Paul Gauguin (1848–1903)

Through the centuries we've seen art for the sake of religion, art for the sake of a patron, and in the nineteenth century, art with a new purpose: art for art's sake! The idea hardly raises an eyebrow today. In Gauguin's time, it was revolutionary.

The political upheavals that rocked Europe after the French Revolution changed the art world, too. The aristocracy who had supported the arts and dictated the painting styles was pretty much wiped out. Now, freed from painting to a patron's taste — and free also to starve and struggle — the artists flew off in many directions to pursue their own personal form of expression. They divided into hostile "schools" and competed for recognition.

One of these fierce individualists was Paul Gauguin. Until the age of thirty-five, he was a fairly prosperous stockbroker in Paris, an amateur painter and a serious art collector. But suddenly his desire to paint overpowered him. He chucked his business, his wife and five children, and spent the rest of his life painting, searching, traveling in many directions — to Brittany in northern France, to Tahiti in the South Seas, to the sun-filled provinces of southern France, and finally back to the South Seas. He was disenchanted with civilization and hoped that, living among simple peasant people, he would find a more direct approach to nature, religion and painting.

While in Brittany, he met up with a young painter, Émile Bernard, who had developed a new approach to painting based on old concepts found in Medieval panels and stained-glass windows. Gauguin was so taken with Bernard's new style that he seized it with a passion. He also steeped himself in further study of primitive art — Persian, Egyptian and Oriental. As a result of all his exposure to early forms, he abandoned the sophisticated teachings of the Renaissance. He eliminated foreshortening, modeling and perspective. He reduced his paintings to flat, brilliantly colored forms outlined in heavy black line. He gave up working directly from nature, but studied and "abstracted" from it. And color was used to convey feeling, not reality. But in spite of his intense concern with the formal elements of his painting, his pictures always convey a meaning beyond their exquisite decorative surfaces. Whether it is a Tahitian mother and child, a group of women bathing or a fisherman at rest beside his boat, the figures are painted in symbolic, primitive attitudes that evoke deeply religious sentiments.

In his later years, his style softened a bit. In the painting used for our needlepoint, *Fatata Te Miti*, painted in 1892, the heavy black outlines gave way to softer lines and somewhat modeled forms. Colors flow in sweeping curves; arbitrary shapes unite with natural forms and create a landscape that is both imaginary and real.

In his frenetic break with tradition and his exhortations to other artists to paint from *within* instead of from nature, Gauguin paved the way for all the nonrepresentational trends of the twentieth century. His thinking and his work influenced Van Gogh, Matisse, Picasso, Braque and other modern giants. It's not without reason that he has been credited with being the creator of modern painting.

The original *Fatata Te Miti* painting is in the National Gallery of Art, Washington, D.C. (the Chester Dale Collection).

The needlepoint sample was worked by Frances Tenenbaum.

Thread Count: 169 × 128

Canvas Gauge	Approximate Size
#18	9½ inches × 7 inches
#14	11⅞ inches × 9⅛ inches
#10	16⅝ inches × 12¼ inches
# 5	33⅝ inches × 25¾ inches

Yellow #457 ○   ∩ #756 *Light blue*

Purplish brown #115 ▦   ● #642 *Purple*

Darkest green #340 \   ✕ #843 *Red*

Dark green #G30 /   ⚡ #968 *Red orange*

Medium green #G32 —   ‖ #126 *Tan*

Light yellow green #592 •   ◤ #283 *Dark pink*

Light blue green #017 φ   ⊙ #423 *Yellow orange*

Black #050 ■   □ #612 *Mauve*

Hot pink #659 ▦

A   B

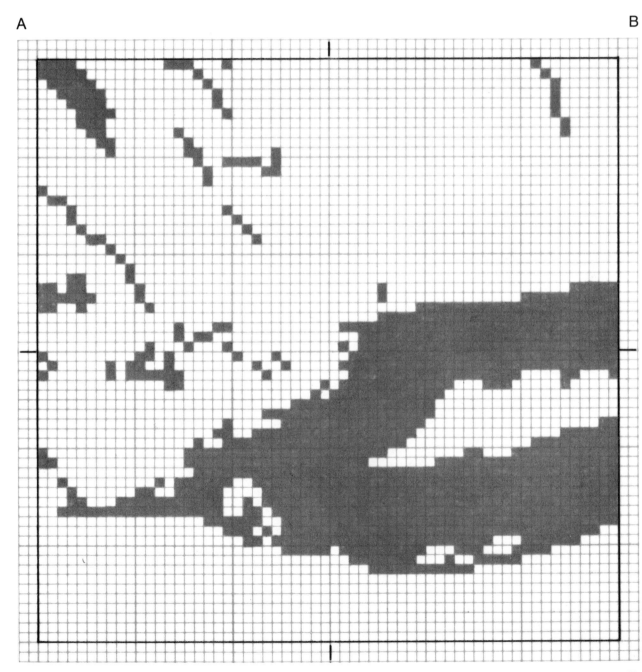

C   D

A

B

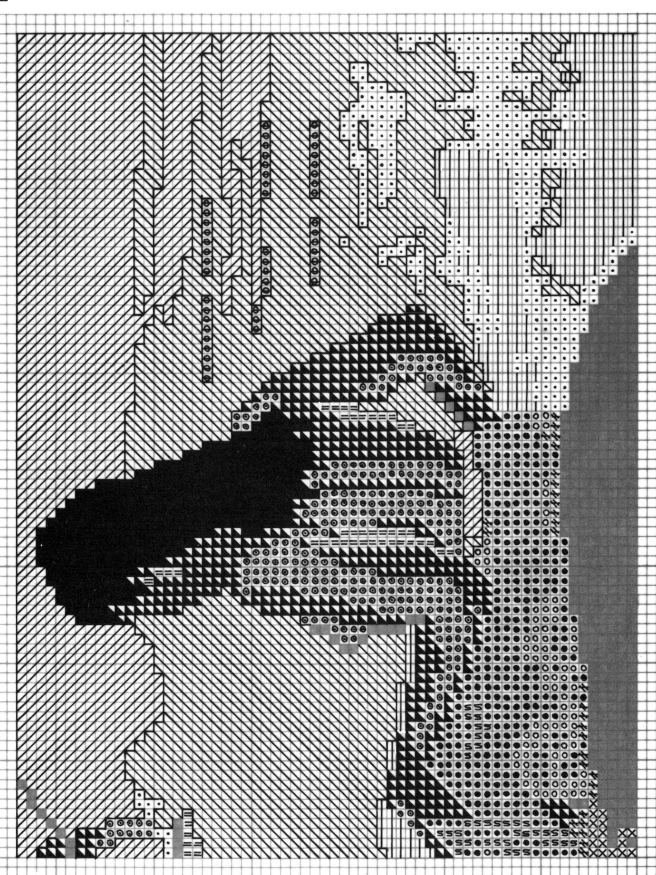

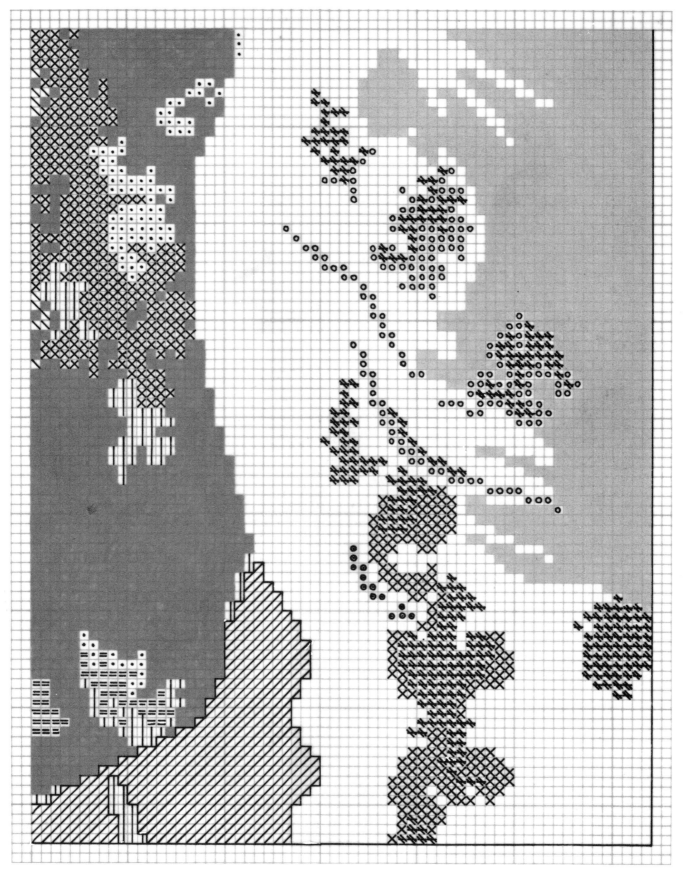

C

Breton Women at Prayer
by Émile Bernard (1868–1941)

This tender but powerful painting, *Breton Women at Prayer*, by Émile Bernard, is very often mistaken for a work by Paul Gauguin. Because their painting styles were so similar, and because Bernard was twenty years younger than Gauguin, it was often assumed that Gauguin was Bernard's teacher. The confusion was the grief of Émile Bernard's life. Actually, there is much evidence that it was Bernard who introduced Gauguin to the ideas behind the Synthetist form of painting — the style that Gauguin adopted and made famous. How did this come about?

From his earliest years, Émile Bernard had a love affair with art. As a very young child, he hung color prints of Medieval paintings over his bed. At the age of twelve, he had already copied a Frans Hals painting in the museum at Lille near his home. Later, as a young man, he enrolled in the Academy in Paris. But he spent more time in the Louvre studying the Old Masters than in the classrooms of the Academy. He also met and fell in with Toulouse-Lautrec and several established Impressionist painters, who gathered in Lautrec's studio to work and discuss ideas that might help them break away from the traditional form of painting practiced since Renaissance times. They were all seeking a more direct, expressive approach to their work.

Bernard actually discovered what he was seeking by rediscovering the masterpieces of the Middle Ages that had appealed to him even as a child. He studied the ancient panels and stained-glass windows and adapted their techniques. Figures were broken into shapes of pure, brilliant color and outlined in heavy black line. He eliminated traditional perspective, foreshortening and atmospheric effects. He gave each element of his painting equal importance in the total design. He departed from the prevailing custom of painting from models and "on location." Instead, he painted from memory, reconstructing and resynthesizing scenes in his studio. Figures became symbols rather than actual people. Trees, mountains and other elements of landscape also appeared more symbolic than real.

Working in this manner, he arrived in Brittany to join the group of artists that had gathered there. It was at precisely the same time that Paul Gauguin abandoned the commercial world and moved to Brittany to live and work among the farm people. Upon seeing Bernard's work, Gauguin was immediately smitten. He recognized the form he was seeking — simple, powerful, direct! Émile Bernard, the young philosophical intellectual, spent hours explaining his color theories and philosophy of painting to Gauguin . . . and Gauguin, the tempestuous, powerful, domineering personality, grabbed the ball and ran with it.

Bernard never forgave Gauguin, or the world, for crediting Gauguin with the invention of Synthetist painting. The truth is that Gauguin, with his energy, intuitive artistry and passion, carried the form to heights the timid Bernard never achieved. Nevertheless, it gives us pleasure to include this handsome work by Émile Bernard in our collection of needlepoint adaptations and give credit where credit is due.

The original of *Breton Women at Prayer*, painted in 1892, is in the Dallas Museum of Fine Arts, Dallas, Texas, a gift of the Museum League.

The needlepoint sample was worked by Jan Lauritzen.

Thread Count: 170 × 122

Canvas Gauge	Approximate Size
#18	9½ inches × 6⅝ inches
#14	12 inches × 8⅝ inches
#10	16⅝ inches × 11½ inches
# 5	33½ inches × 24⅜ inches

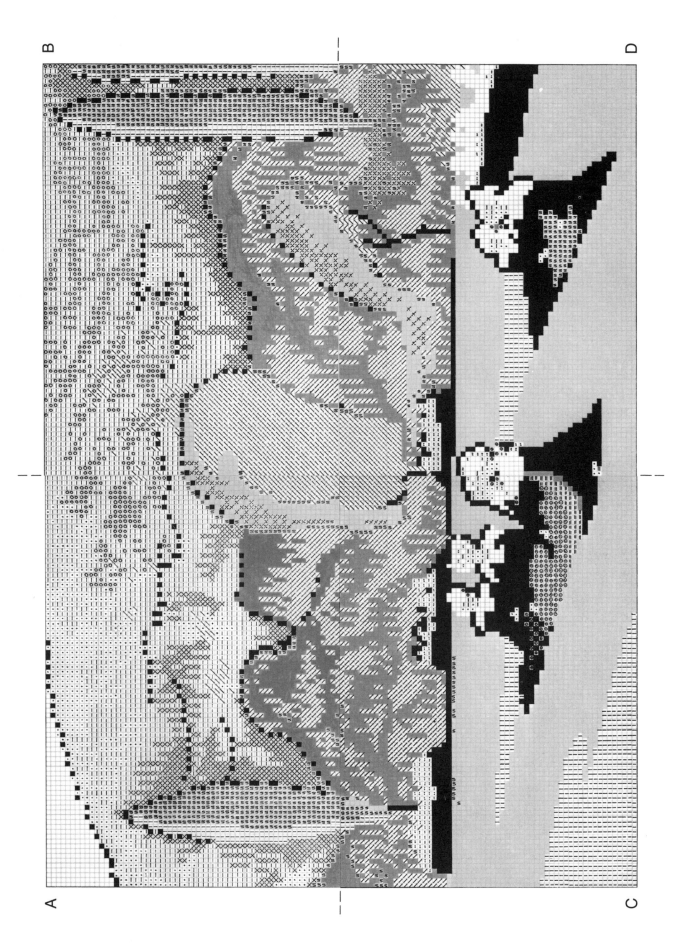

Yellow #455	│	••	#781	Pale blue
Ochre #466	⼹	—	#255	Medium pink
Light pink #265	•	═	#223	Maroon
Wine #115	■	○	#593	Pale yellow green
Medium green #532	▦	⦂̸	#542	Yellow green
Dark green #530	╱	╲	#342	Dark blue green
Dark blue #355	⊙	✕	#843	Red
Medium blue green #352	▦	□	#012	White

A　　　　　　　　　　　　　　　　　　　　　B

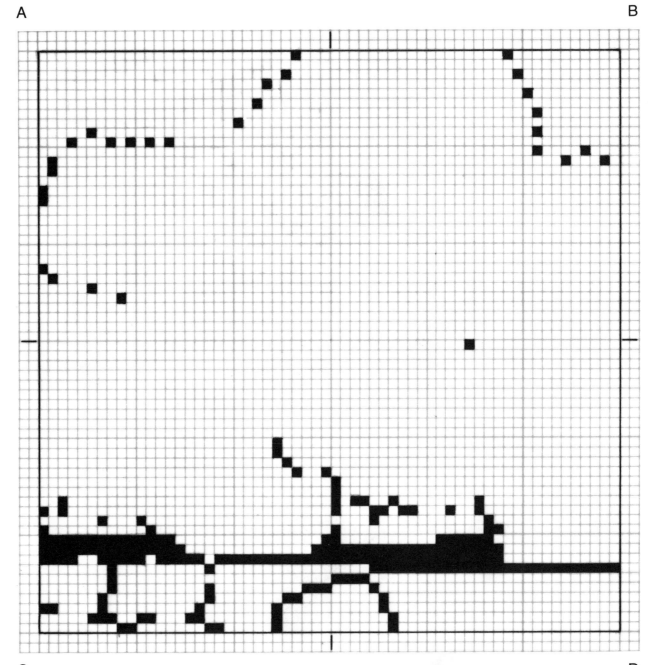

C　　　　　　　　　　　　　　　　　　　　　D

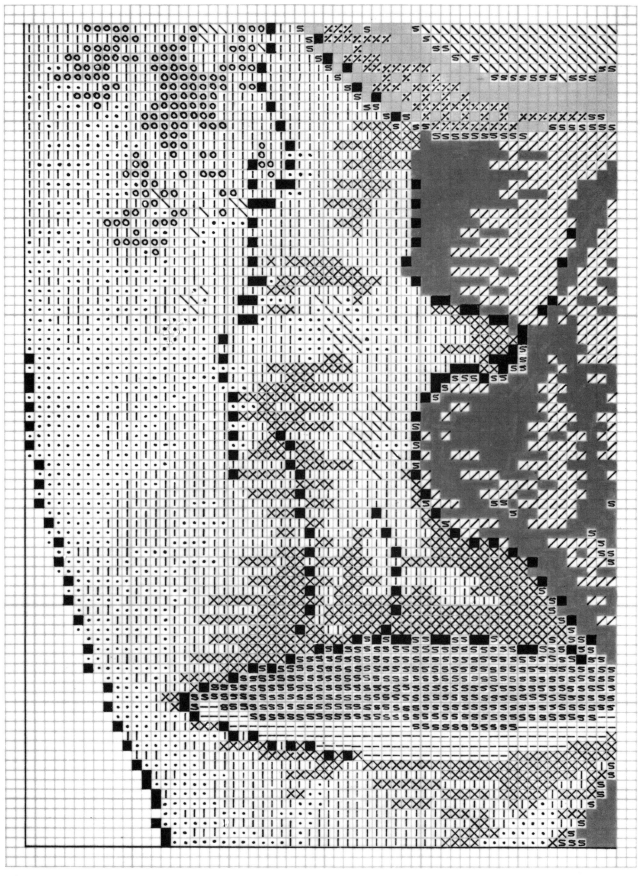

A

B

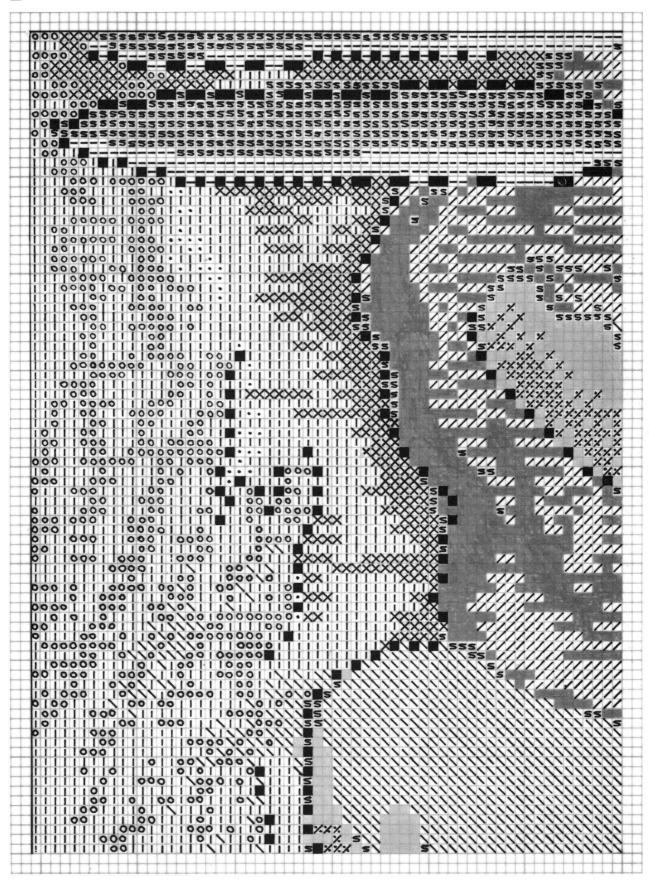

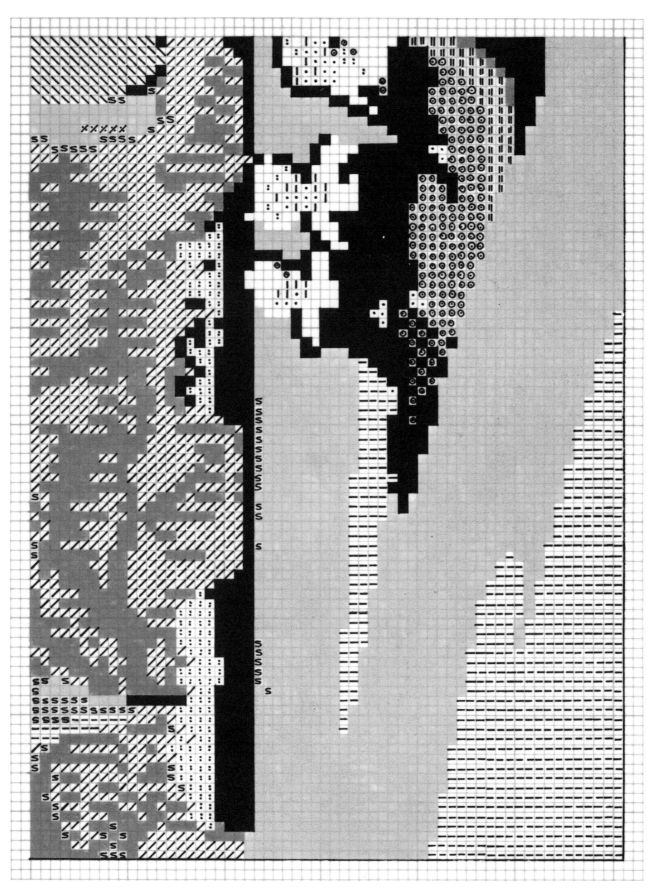

C

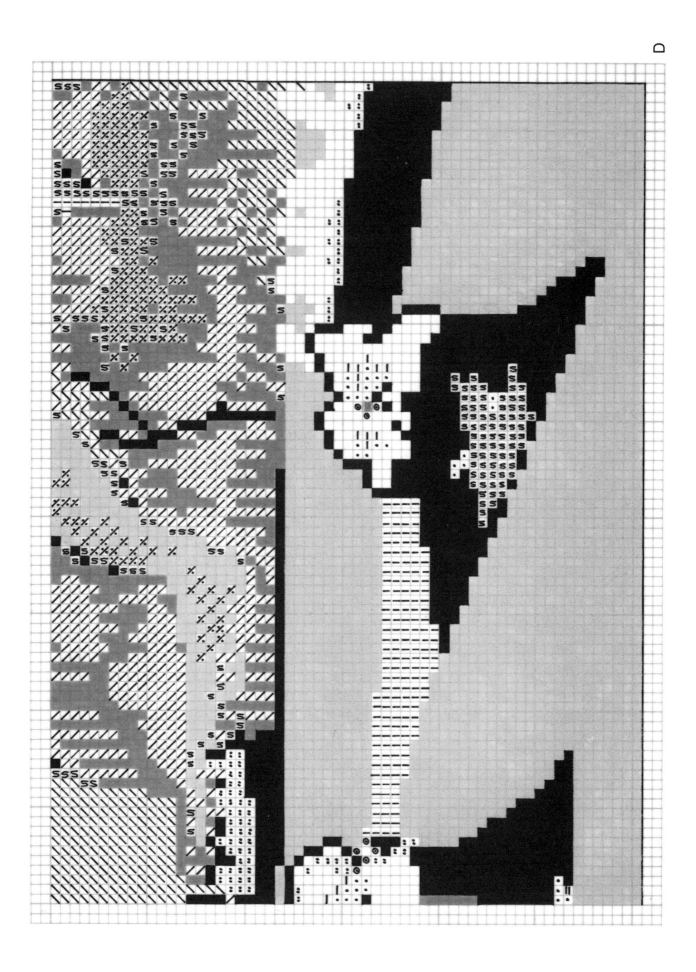

L'Arlésienne

by Vincent van Gogh (1853–1890)

There were two tremendous passions in Vincent van Gogh's brief life: his religion and his art. Actually, it's fair to say that it was his basically pathological personality that drove him to extremes in both these areas — and made him a great artist and a desperate man.

As a young man, he started to study for the ministry, but soon gave that up to become a lay preacher in a small mining town in Belgium. He lived a saintly existence there and was fanatic in his devotion to his parishioners. But his often compulsive and bizarre behavior was troublesome to these simple people, and the ministry did not quell his raging need for an expressive outlet. Fortunately for the world, he retired from religious life and took to drawing and painting. This was not a surprising venture for a Van Gogh. The family had been involved in the art world for a long time, as dealers and agents, and Vincent had had a long exposure to the arts. But rather than buoy him up, it only made him keenly aware of his lack of skills and his mediocrity. The frustration caused him to pursue painting and drawing with the same demonic fervor he had expended in his religious experience.

In ten years — and that was the entire span of his artistic career — he produced 900 paintings and 100 drawings and watercolors!

In France, where he spent almost all of his painting years, he became tremendously interested in the Impressionists' experiments with light and color. But his own blazing drive and frantic insecurity led him to a much more expressive form of painting. It shows up in his persevering brush strokes and his heavy, compulsive laying on of paint. It was precisely his lack of polished skills that gave his painting the strength and vigor for which he is famous.

In the painting L'Arlésienne, from which our needlepoint was adapted, he departed from his more familiar nervous brush style and shows the influence of his fellow painter

and sometime friend Paul Gauguin. The two of them —
volatile and manic personalities — had fierce disputes that
were physical as well as ideological. But they respected and
influenced each other greatly. Gauguin, who was very
much involved with primitive and Oriental art, especially
Japanese woodcuts, had started to paint in flat, simple
forms, bright color and clearly defined outlines.
L'Arlésienne not only shows this influence, but it is almost
an exact replica of a figure in a Gauguin painting of the same
period.

The irony of Van Gogh's life story is that it was a keenly
rational Vincent van Gogh who committed himself to a
mental asylum and finally took his own life when he real-
ized that his manic personality was interfering with his
ability to paint. For him, without his art, life was not worth
living.

The original of *L'Arlésienne* was painted in 1888, two years
before Van Gogh's death. It is in the collection of the Metropolitan Museum of Art, New York City.

The needlepoint sample was worked by Flavia Stutz.

Thread Count: 120 × 157

Canvas Gauge	Approximate Size
#18	6¾ inches × 8½ inches
#14	8½ inches × 11¼ inches
#10	11¾ inches × 14⅞ inches
# 5	23¾ inches × 31½ inches

A   B

C   D

White #005 **=**   • #182 Light blue gray

Pale green #597 ▨ || #520 Green

Pale pink #014 ○   — #516 Dark green

Light orange #425 \   ■ #112 Dark brown

Dusty orange #194 //   / #180 Medium blue gray

Dark orange #414 ✕ | #304 Navy blue

Tan #025 ▨   □ #437 Yellow

Orange #426 ●

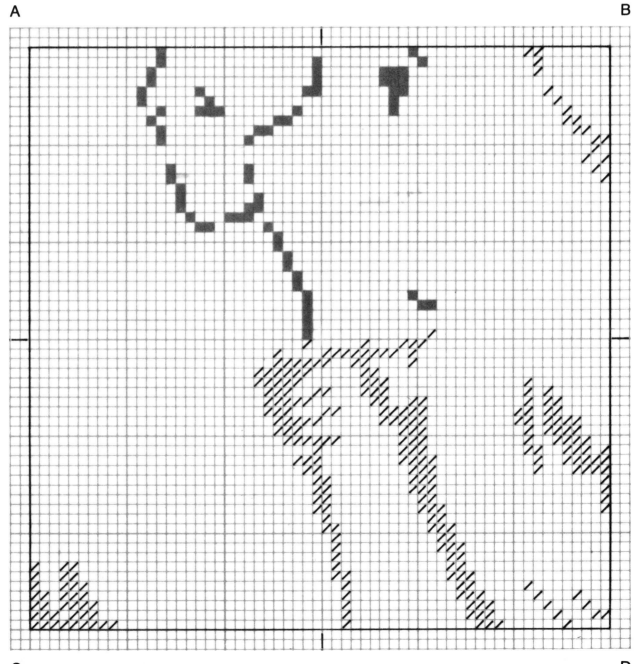

A

B

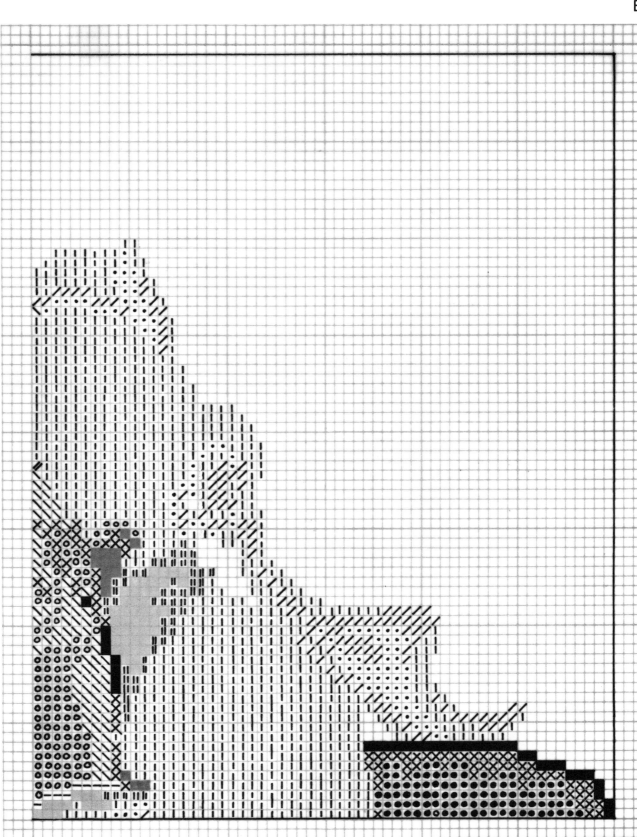

C

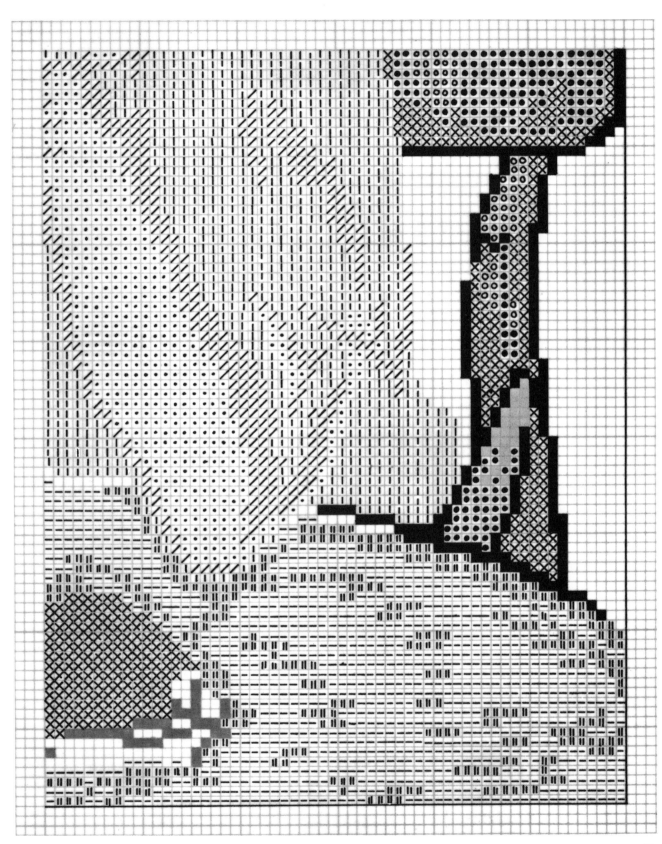

D

Les Poissons

by Georges Braque (1882–1963)

Anyone who knew him as a private citizen would find it hard to believe that the humble, gentle, meditative man Georges Braque was capable of setting the art world on its ear. But in the space of four years, he and Pablo Picasso changed the course of twentieth-century painting in Europe.

They invented Cubism!

Cubism, born in the early 1900s, was a total break with all the teachings and practices handed down since Renaissance times. Although painters like Manet, Cézanne, Gauguin, Van Gogh and others had already broken through many traditional barriers, it was the Cubists who lashed out with a fury and created a whole new set of rules for painting. They condemned the trickery and illusion of traditional painting. It was a "lie," they said, to use perspective and atmospheric effects to represent *deep* space on a *flat* canvas. It was also a lie to use shading and modeling to create illusions of three-dimensional objects on a perfectly flat surface. The object of Cubism was to respect totally the two-dimensional nature of painting . . . and to present a new kind of reality.

Instead of placing objects in infinite space, as in traditional paintings, they brought them up close to the viewer in carefully defined shallow space. All the elements in a picture were reduced to flat planes. To show relative distances, the planes were placed side by side, overlapping, or above or below one another. In analyzing an object or form, they showed not only what *appeared to the eye* at a given time, but what they *knew to be true* of the object at all times. Not just the front view of a pitcher, but the top, bottom and sides, simultaneously. Not just the profile of a head with a single eye, but also the full-view head, with both eyes, superimposed on the profile! It was not important to the Cubists that a subject retain its identity. The whole canvas was their subject. Objects merged with one another and the surrounding space, making individual form sometimes unrecognizable, and the picture an analytic abstraction of the real subject. This phase was called Analytic Cubism.

In the following years, Braque and Picasso reverted to a more personal and legible style of Cubism. They evolved the collage and papier collé technique — using found objects and shapes cut out of precolored paper, which they then assembled to make a picture. The idea of cutting shapes out of paper delighted their appetite for reducing everything to flat planes. Instead of breaking down objects into component planes as in the earlier Analytic phase, they now began to construct or "synthesize" forms out of a variety of materials and shapes of flat color. This new system was called Synthetic Cubism and the painting *Les Poissons* (*The Fish*) is typical of the period. The fish are simple flat black shapes. The dish is a flat gray oval. The table is a black semicircle. The wall is a flat saffron-colored rectangle. Yet each element takes its place in the picture. There is no question that the fish are lying on the platter, the platter sits on the table, and the table is in front of the wall.

Braque's special contribution to Cubism grew out of his background and skill as a house painter. He was adept at mixing materials into his paints and varnishes to build unusual surface textures. He mixed sand, sawdust and even metal filings into his colors. He was also skilled at imitating wood-grain and marble surfaces. In the flat, flat painting style of the Cubists, Braque's textural innovations became an important device for differentiating closely related planes. His inventiveness also opened the door for others to dare to cross the threshold of what is permissible in fine art.

The original of *Les Poissons,* painted in 1942, is in the collection of the Musée National d'Art Moderne, Paris.

The needlepoint sample was worked by Marion Muller.

Thread Count: 169 × 106

Canvas Gauge	Approximate Size
#18	9½ inches × 5½ inches
#14	11⅞ inches × 7½ inches
#10	16⅝ inches × 10 inches
# 5	33⅝ inches × 21¼ inches

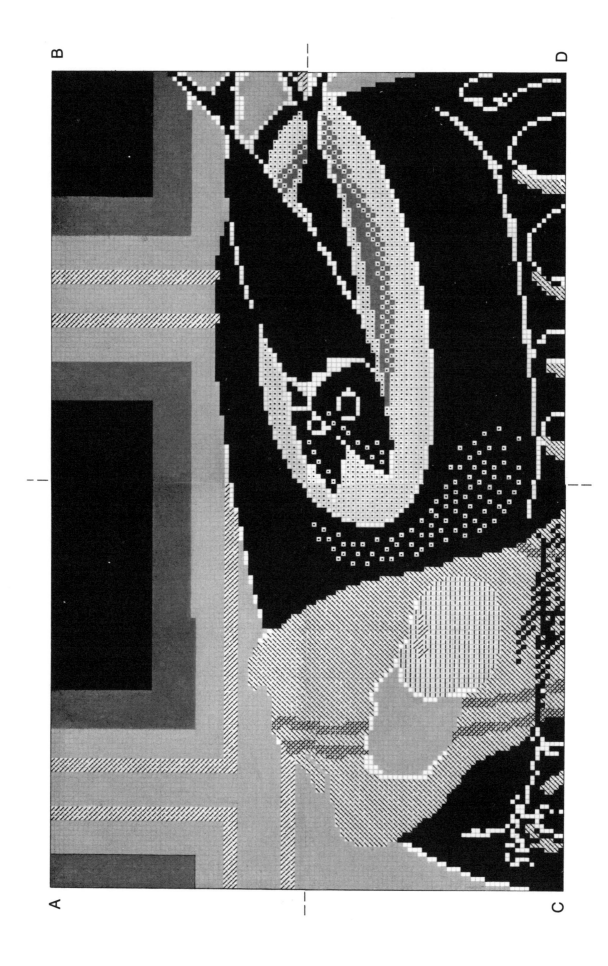

Orange	#454	—	/	#392	*Blue gray*
Red	#852	✕	▨	#455	*Pale ochre*
Light gray	#168	•	\	#466	*Ochre*
Medium gray	#164	▦	☐	#005	*White*
Dark gray	#108	■			

A   B

C   D

A

B

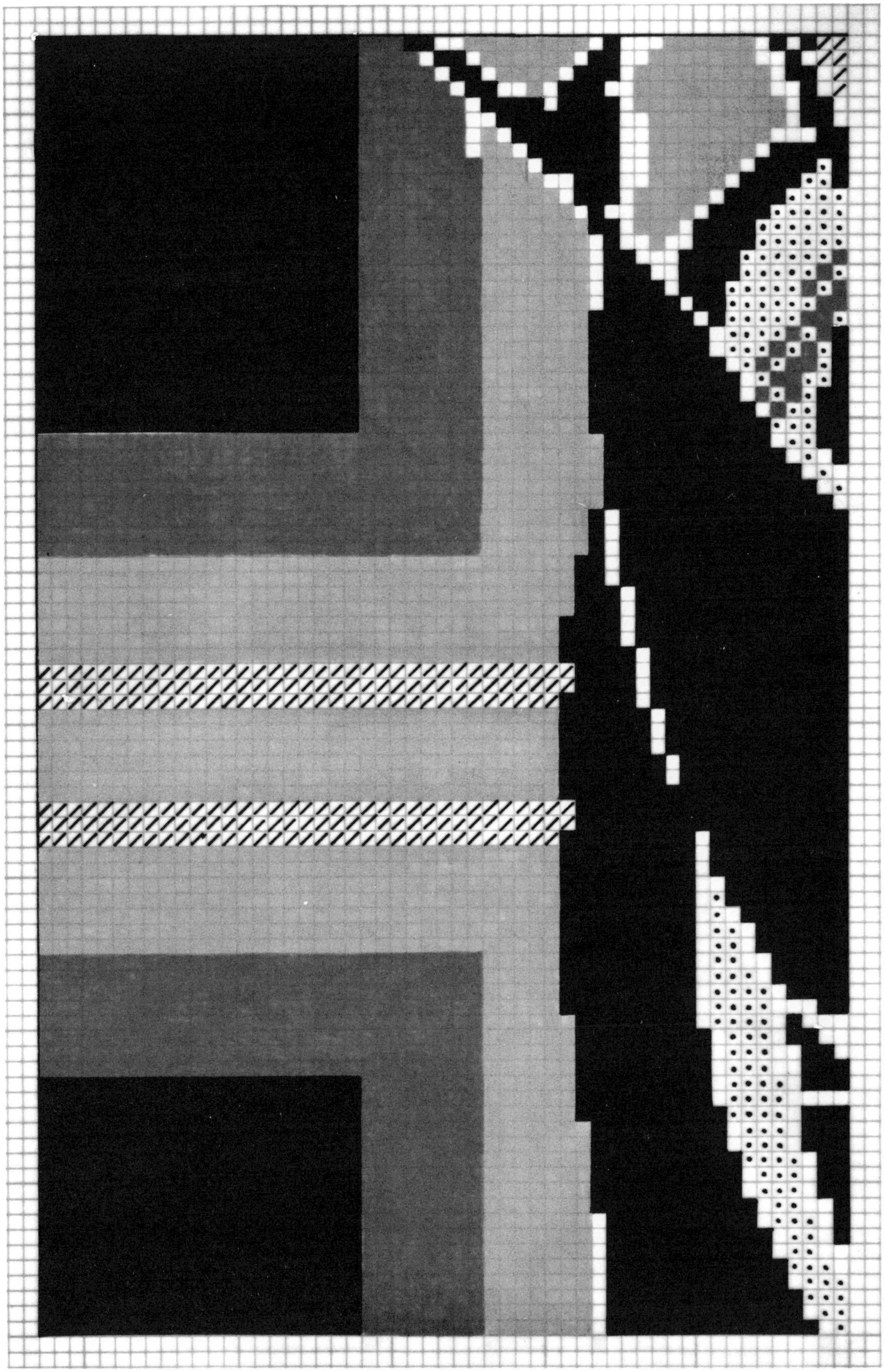

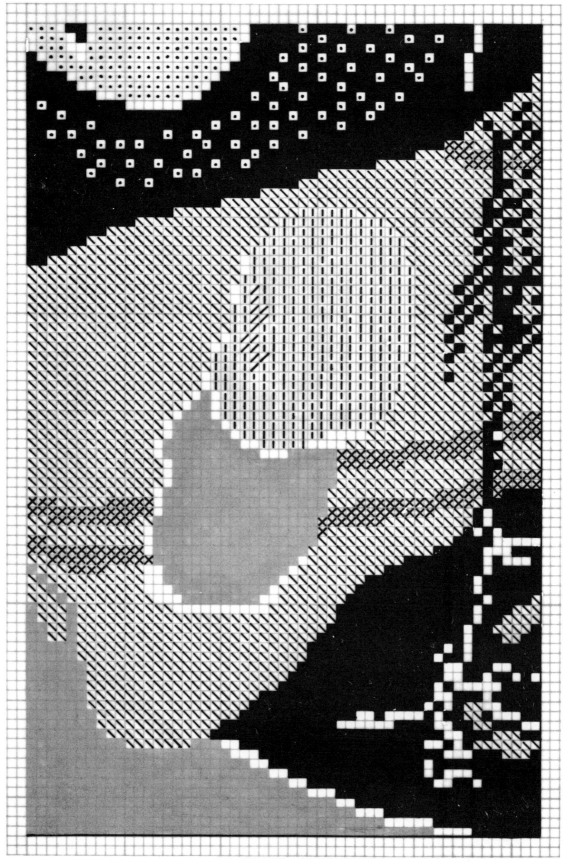

C

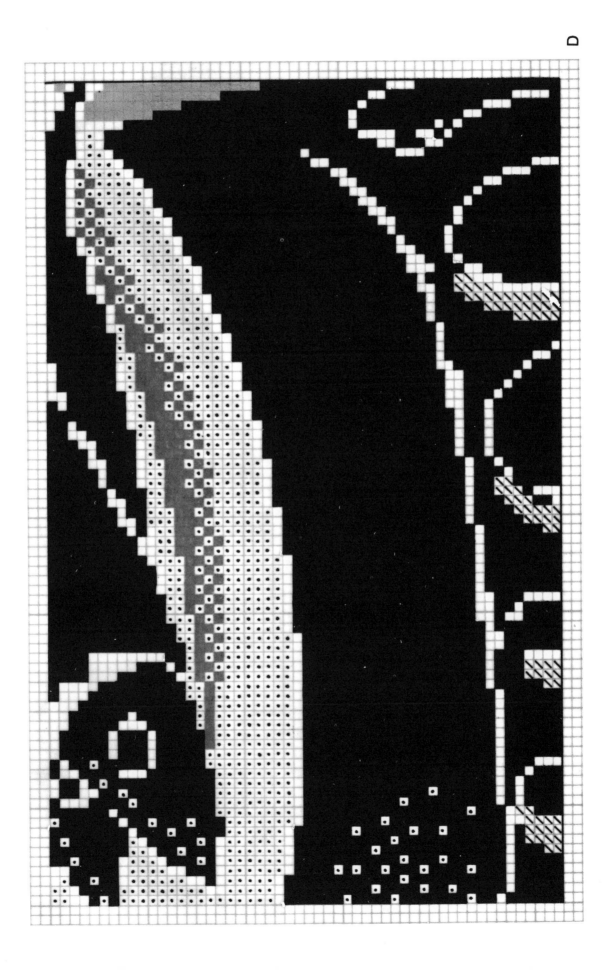

Dance

by Henri Matisse (1869–1954)

"He was born to simplify painting." That was the prediction made by a famous painter and teacher, Gustave Moreau, of his even more famous pupil, Henri Matisse.

The fact is, during the first twenty years of his life, there was not the slightest hint of Henri Matisse's artistic inclination. He was actually engaged in a successful but stuffy legal career when he suffered a bout with appendicitis that kept him in bed for a long time. During the tedious convalescence, his mother bought him a set of paints and an instruction book to help him pass the time. The effect on the young man was stunning. He took to painting with a passion. His entire prior existence became meaningless. He felt as if his art "led him" — a strange romantic reaction from someone who had, until then, led a controlled and disciplined life.

His lack of formal art training troubled him, so he steeped himself in studying the works of antiquity and the Old Masters. He visited exotic places and opened himself to all their influences. The colors and patterns of the Islamic and Oriental worlds permeated his work. He did not follow any special theories or school of painting, but proceeded in an intuitive way. His method was to draw and paint the same subject over and over again — abstracting, reducing, purifying — until he could finally set down the very essence of an idea.

In *Dance,* painted in 1909, Matisse's major powers as a painter became clear. He eliminated all illusionistic devices — modeling, shading, atmospheric effects, even the flat overlapping planes of the Cubist painters — and relied on simple line, pure color and the total unity of the figures, color and background to express the joy of dance. While his form was new, his source was the rich treasure of the past. The dancing ladies derive from the graceful flowing figures one finds on ancient Greek vases. Even the color in the final version of *Dance,* which hangs in the Hermitage museum in the Soviet Union, is the same rich red ochre color found in Greek pottery. The hands of the dancers in the foreground reach toward each other with the same grace and tension as the hands in Michelangelo's *Creation.*

In spite of the intensity of Matisse's studies, his goal was to make his paintings look spontaneous and joyous. He wanted no one to suspect the labor and effort involved. He did indeed, as his teacher prophesied, simplify painting.

There are two versions of the painting *Dance.* One hangs in the Museum of Modern Art, New York City, a gift of Nelson A. Rockefeller, in honor of Alfred Barr. The other is in the collection of the Hermitage museum, Leningrad.

The needlepoint sample was worked by Brande Ormond.

Thread Count: 170 × 115

Canvas Gauge	Approximate Size
#18	9½ inches × 6¼ inches
#14	12 inches × 8⅛ inches
#10	16⅝ inches × 10¾ inches
# 5	33½ inches × 23 inches

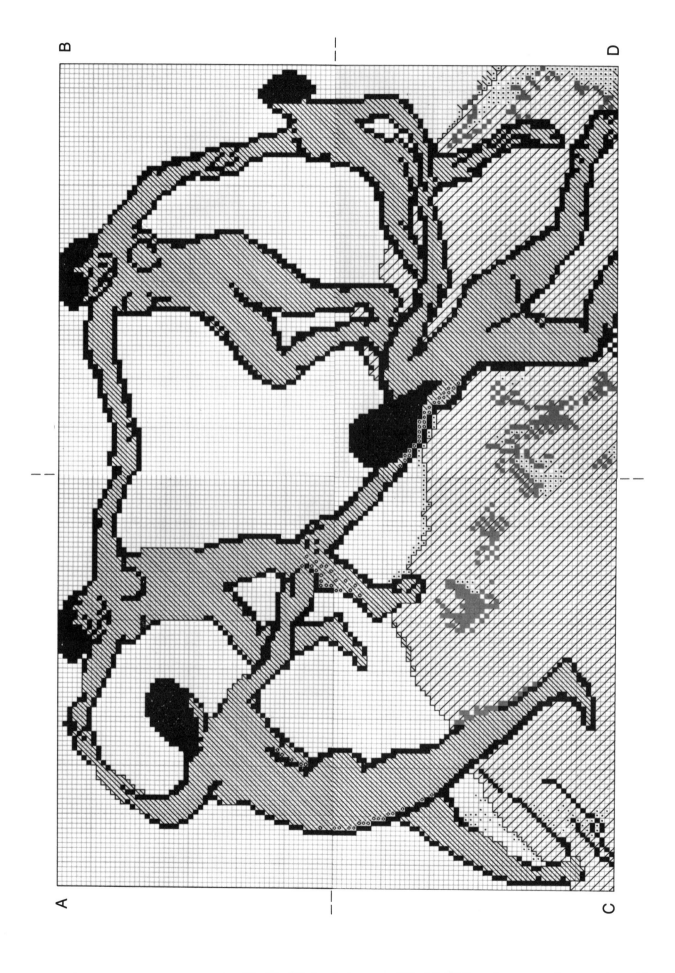

Green #524 ◨

Flesh #287 ◪

Dark brown #110 ■

Orange #434 ○

• #641 *Lavender*

■ #755 *Teal*

□ #752 *Blue*

A B

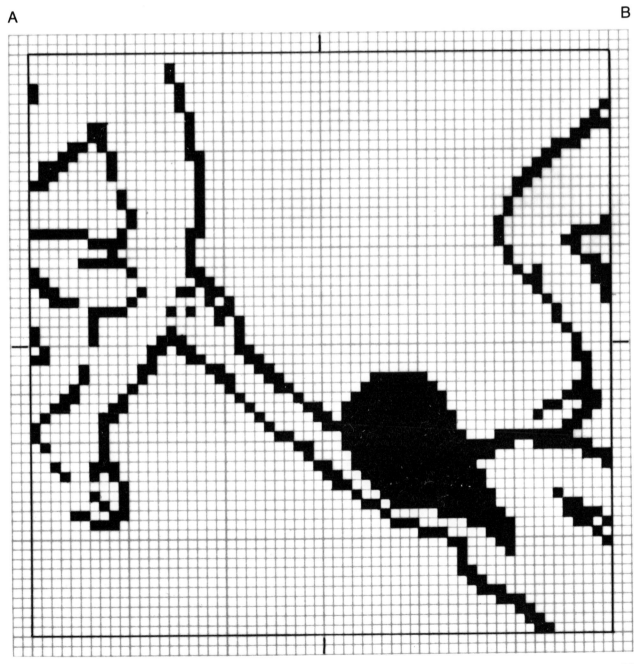

C D

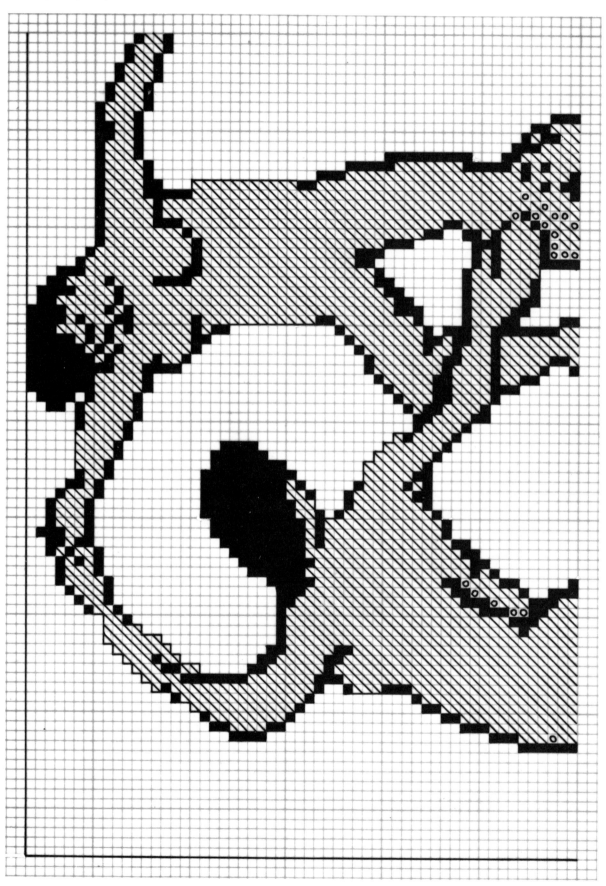

A

B

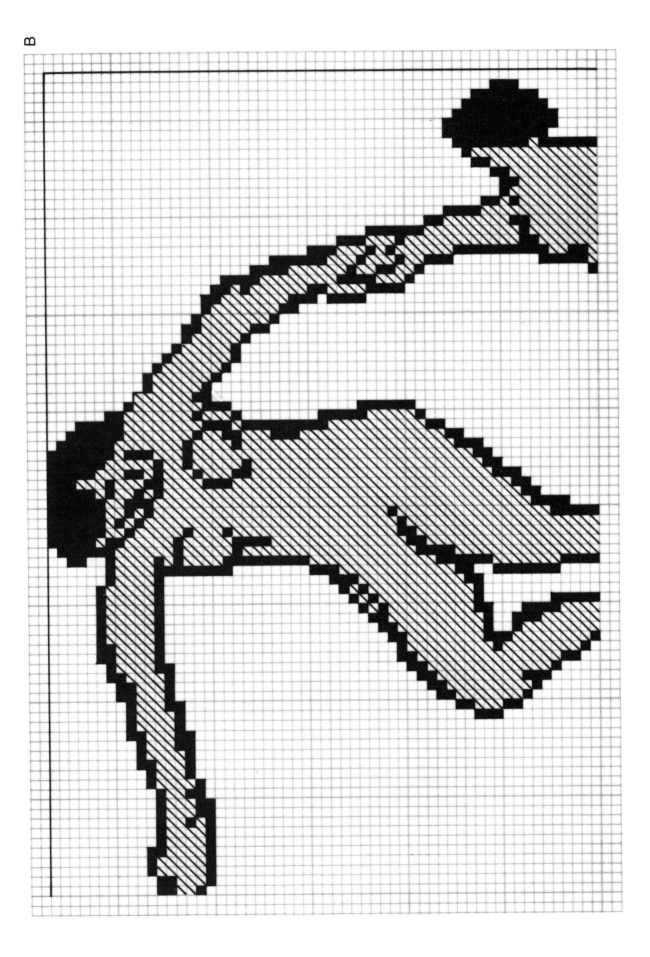

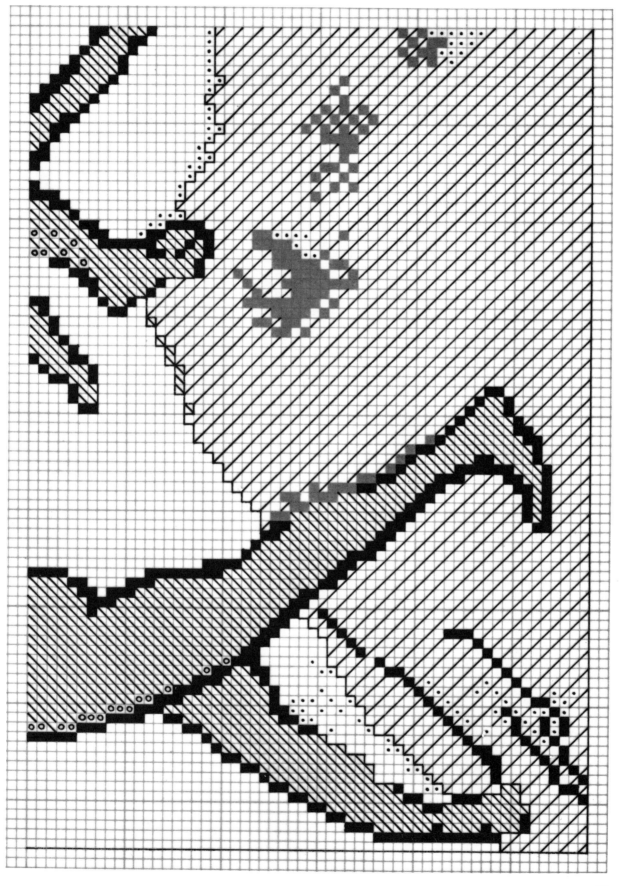

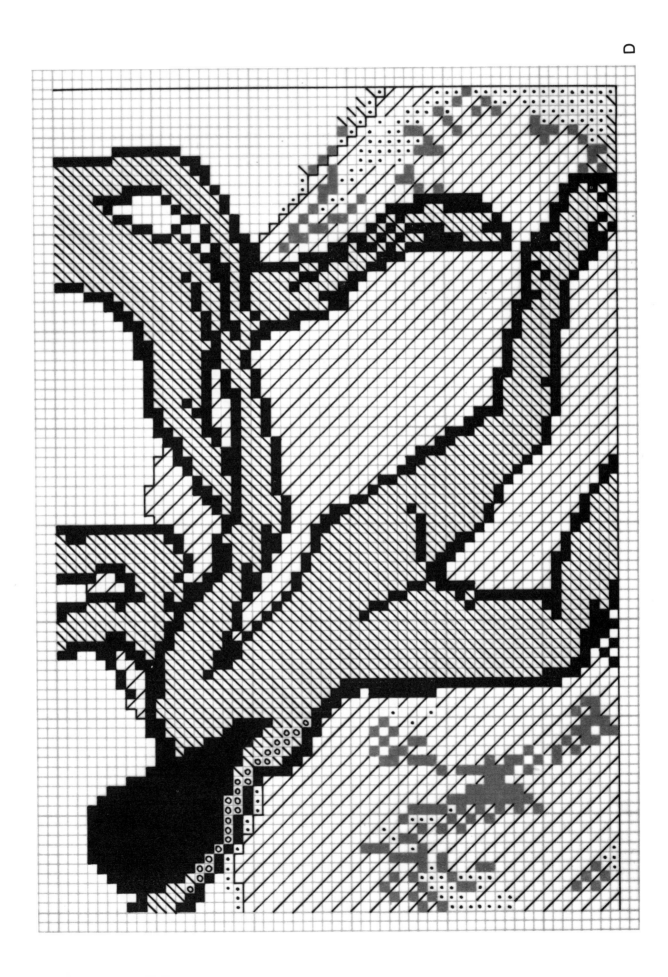

Ivy in Flower
by Henri Matisse (1869–1954)

Someone once poignantly observed that Matisse's artistic career started in bed . . . and ended in bed. (The story of his convalescence from appendicitis and his first painting experience has been described in the previous section on Matisse.) In the final years of his life, when he was in his eighties, another intestinal ailment made him so feeble that he became a virtual prisoner of his own bed. But his physical confinement in no way restrained his soaring creative spirit.

Years before, he had experimented, like the Cubists, with a technique of cutting forms out of precolored paper and arranging them into a picture. He liked the idea of coloring his own paper; he could obtain exactly the hue he visualized. He liked the directness and honesty of cutting a shape solely with his scissors; it ruled out accident and indecisiveness. Now, confined to bed and unable to paint at an easel, this technique, called gouache découpé (gouache, referring to the kind of water-soluble paint he used, and découpé, meaning cutout), became a necessity and a triumph.

His scissors became his drawing tool and his paintbrush. He reveled in the joy of cutting directly into color — like a sculptor carving directly into his material. It also brought him closer to his urgent goal: to simplify. Previously his forms were objects in the complicated space of a total picture. Now his cutouts were simple signs or emblems of objects — and that was quite enough for him!

Matisse used this gouache découpé technique from 1950 until his death in 1954. *Ivy in Flower,* which he created in 1953, was one of a series of flower forms, leaves, dancers, swimmers and acrobats that flowed from his memory directly into paper — a joyous and tender outpouring of his feelings about nature, life and art.

The original of *Ivy in Flower* is in the Dallas Museum of Fine Arts, Foundation for the Arts Collection, a gift of the Albert and Mary Lasker Foundation.

The needlepoint sample was worked by Alberta Saletan.

Thread Count: 140 × 143

Canvas Gauge	Approximate Size
#18	7⅞ inches × 7¾ inches
#14	9⅞ inches × 10⅛ inches
#10	13¾ inches × 13½ inches
# 5	27⅝ inches × 28½ inches

A

B

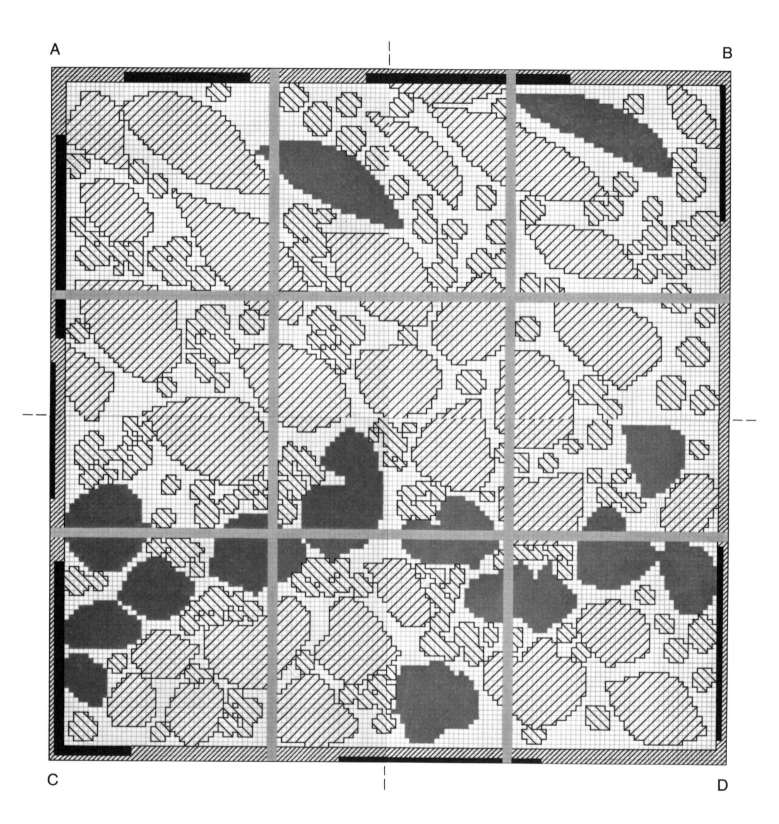

C

D

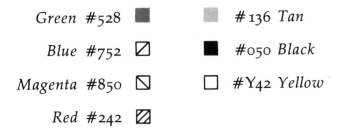

Green #528 ■   #136 *Tan*

Blue #752 ◪   #050 *Black*

Magenta #850 ◨   #Y42 *Yellow*

Red #242 ◪

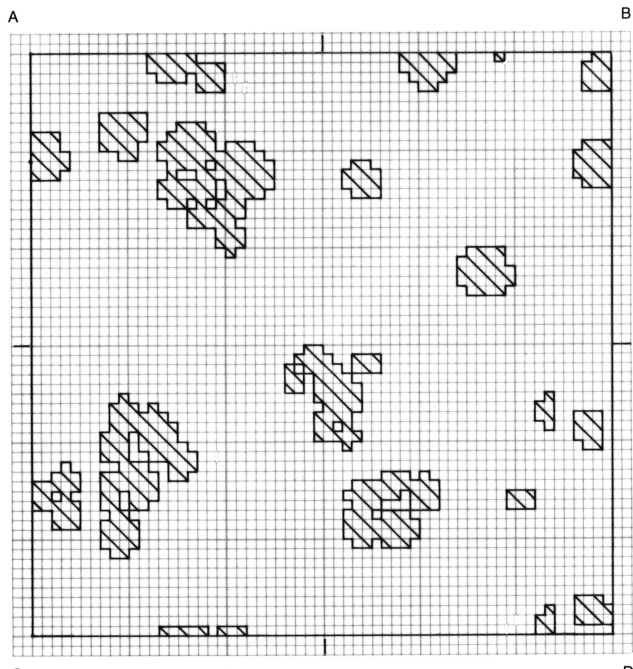

A   B

C   D

A

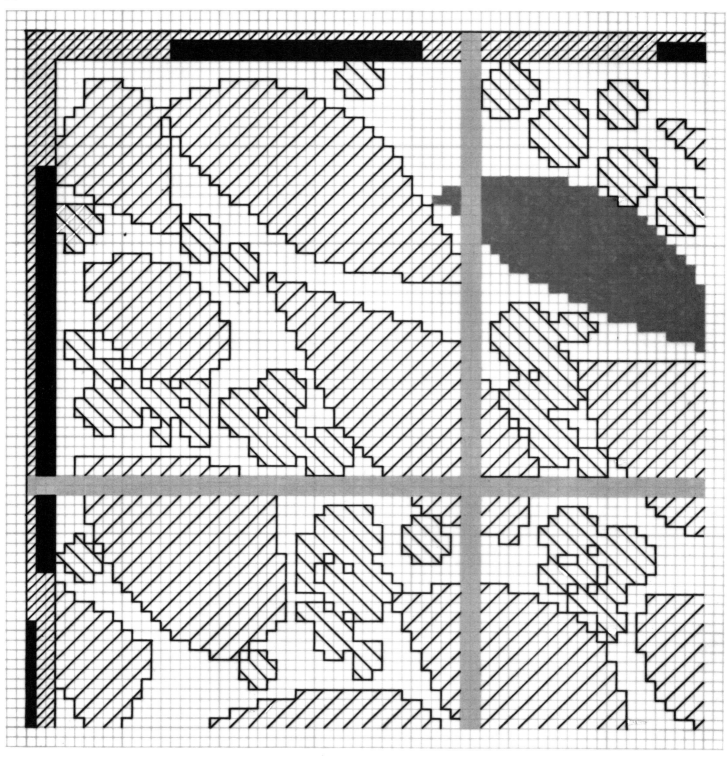

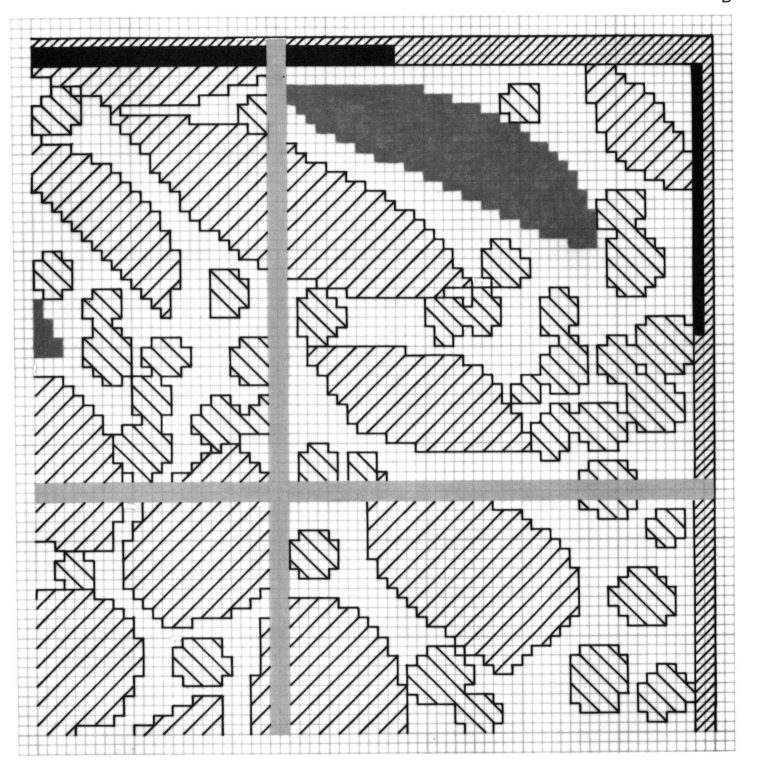

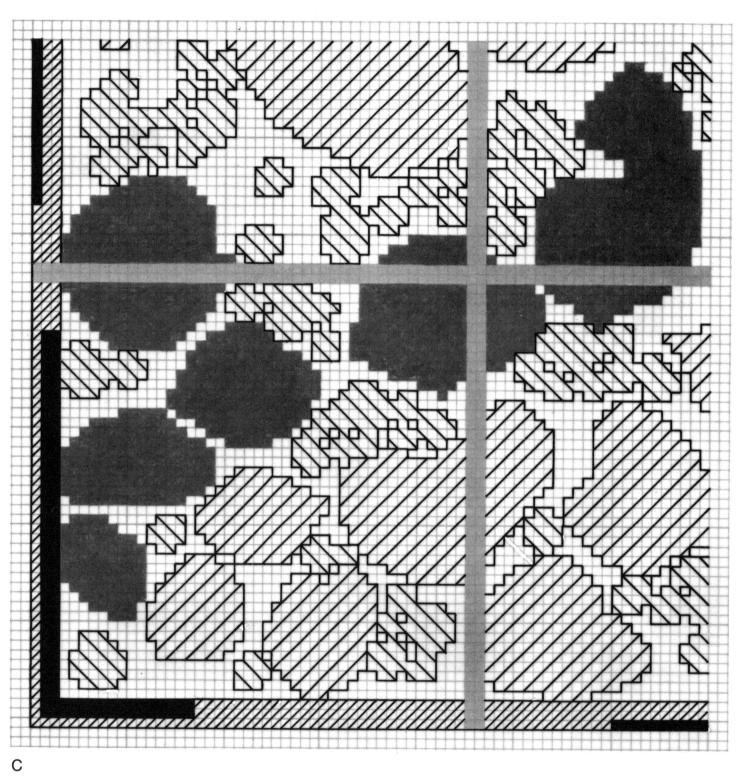

C